"Spiritual formation with substance and depth! Alex Sosler gives a thick account of Christian growth in holiness and wholeness shaped by a biblical-theological-ecclesial vision of truth, goodness, beauty, and community. Anyone who's sung the Augustinian cri de coeur of Bono's 'I still haven't found what I'm looking for' but found the modern spiritual formation literature too light and fluffy will be glad for this winsome retrieval of classical theology in service to a practice of discipleship that can take shape in real communities. This is one to read, mark, learn, and inwardly digest and then share with another pilgrim on the way of the restless heart."

—**Alex Fogleman**, Institute for Studies of Religion, Baylor University; director, Catechesis Institute; author of *Knowledge, Faith, and Early Christian Initiation*

"*A Short Guide to Spiritual Formation* is a true retrieval, rooting Christian practice in the wider Christian tradition while remaining attentive to the needs and questions of the present moment. This fresh account of Christian spiritual formation will captivate students and seekers while reminding seasoned leaders of the many gifts that the Christian tradition offers to our weary souls."

—**Kaitlyn Schiess**, author of *The Ballot and the Bible: How Scripture Has Been Used and Abused in American Politics and Where We Go from Here*

"This book will be a great help to anyone interested in personal and corporate spiritual formation. The rich traditions of the church are beneficial for modern-day disciples. It is important to know our spiritual history and some of the key foundations that Christian faith rests upon. Sosler does a masterful job of describing these historical, theological, and spiritual foundations, and in doing so he invites the reader into a deeper relationship with God. This text is well worth your time."

—**Donald Shepson**, Grove City College

"Sosler provides readers with a theological, historical, contemplative, and applicable approach to living life from a formative perspective. He is passionate about the well-being of God's creation and implementing practices designed to educate, empower, and equip the learne͟ ͟ ͟ ͟ ts and tradition' and writes about ͟ ͟ ͟ ͟ o Christianity than 'just the way tl

L. Peacock, Peacock Soul Care

✳ A ✳
SHORT GUIDE
to
SPIRITUAL
FORMATION

FINDING LIFE IN TRUTH, GOODNESS, BEAUTY, AND COMMUNITY

ALEX SOSLER

FOREWORD BY RUSSELL MOORE

𝕭

Baker Academic

a division of Baker Publishing Group
Grand Rapids, Michigan

© 2024 by Alex Sosler

Published by Baker Academic
a division of Baker Publishing Group
Grand Rapids, Michigan
BakerAcademic.com

Printed in the United States of America

Library of Congress Cataloging-in-Publication Data
Names: Sosler, Alex, 1989– author.
Title: A short guide to spiritual formation : finding life in truth, goodness, beauty, and community / Alex Sosler.
Description: Grand Rapids, Michigan : Baker Academic, a division of Baker Publishing Group, 2024. | Includes bibliographical references and index.
Identifiers: LCCN 2023040909 | ISBN 9781540966612 (paperback) | ISBN 9781540967855 (casebound) | ISBN 9781493446353 (ebook) | ISBN 9781493446360 (pdf)
Subjects: LCSH: Spiritual formation.
Classification: LCC BV4501.3 .S6595 2024 | DDC 248.4—dc23/eng/20231122
LC record available at https://lccn.loc.gov/2023040909

Cover design by Paula Gibson

Baker Publishing Group publications use paper produced from sustainable forestry practices and postconsumer waste whenever possible.

24 25 26 27 28 29 30   7 6 5 4 3 2 1

To Mariela, Auden, and Jude

While researching this book, I watched you play on the front porch. I read while I put you down for bed and as I waited in the school pickup line. I paused my work to break up your fights or console you. In my worst moments I viewed these interruptions as distractions that kept me from an otherwise happy, peaceful, and quiet life. But more and more, I've come to see the blessings of a loud, boisterous, and interrupted life. This book has my children's handprints (and spills) all over it. You are blessed interruptions. *I love being your dad.*

CONTENTS

Foreword

I once knew a man who would end every conversation with the words "Be good." At first, I found this odd. After all, "Be good" is what a mother might say to her child as she sends that child off the first day of school or to summer camp; it's not usually what friends and coworkers say to each other at the end of a phone call or after a visit in the aisle of a grocery store. For him, though, it filled the place that "Aloha" would in Hawaii or "Come see us" would in my hometown— a kind way to signal well wishes at the end of a talk. Most of us don't say "Be good" to acquaintances in any context, though, in some sense, that's exactly what we expect and hope. We want the people around us to be faithful, responsible, and honest. When you think of your own flaws, you may well find a way to justify them or to contextualize them or even ignore them. But I would almost guarantee that none of you ever started down a wrong path in life by saying to yourself, "I am setting out on a journey to vice." In some sense, we all want to pursue goodness, but often we have no idea how to do so. And sometimes, we are confused about what "good" even means.

That's not just a problem for us with our behavior. For those of us who are Christians, it's also often an internal skirmish when it comes to what some people call the "spiritual disciplines." For lots of us, prayer and contemplation and Bible reading are hard. We find our attention distracted or the clocks whirling by with activities, and we wonder, "How do other people do this with such ease? What's wrong with me?" We add to that our lives together in churches. Some people wonder, "Am I really a good church member since I just don't know how to get to know people, much less what gifts I would have with which to serve?"

This book by Alex Sosler is not a guilt-inducing to-do list from a guru or a "life coach." Instead, this book helps us to think through just what's in the way of our pursuit of virtue—or, better, of Christ-likeness. The book doesn't hit us with abstractions but with specific, concrete counsel on how to recognize and to pursue truth, goodness, beauty, and community. You will not leave this short book burdened down with a sense of all the things you can't ever seem to do. You'll instead start to see the possibility of how you, in your own life, can seek holiness and formation. The book neither leaves us with an exhausting and counter-gospel legalism nor with an exhausting and counter-gospel sloth. The author knows that we don't ascend the ladder to God by performing better with our prayers or our works. God has come to us, and the Ladder has a name, Jesus of Nazareth. The sort of obedience we seek starts with freedom, not with indebtedness.

Be good.

Russell Moore

Introduction

I search for rest in all the wrong places.

I've sought rest in ambitious success, in getting things done. I've thought that after the next accomplishment, things will slow down, and then I'll be happy. I've sought rest in family harmony. After this move, after a child gets to such and such age, then I'll be satisfied. After this experience, I can settle down. Peace is always around the corner. I've sought satiation in financial stability. Once I get so much money, then I will rest. Like the child in the book *The Giving Tree* by Shel Silverstein, who uses all of a tree's resources—apples, limbs, and trunk—until it's a mere stump, I use all of life, abusing good gifts, all in search of happiness.

As I look out into the world, I see the same restlessness at work. Wars are fought with the drive for more: more land, more oil, more resources, more people. Conflict comes with unhinged desires: I want what I want when I want it, and this person is keeping me from my desire. I see people with passionate resolve that leads to pain in themselves and in others. I see young people longing for affirmation, for someone to notice them, for someone to like them.

I'm surrounded by restless craving. We all have hidden hungers.

What about you? What do you want? What are you seeking? How's that going?

Perhaps you thought a relationship with the opposite sex would bring you happiness. But you end up stuck or broken if that relationship fails. So, you try more relationships, thinking that may do the trick. But after each new fling, you feel more destitute than before.

Or maybe you have sought satisfaction in earning the best grades and being the smartest in the room. And all that learning made you feel more insecure, like you would never be smart enough, never good enough.

Ronald Rolheiser observes, "Spirituality is what we do with our unrest."[1] Either this searching leads to greater integration with God, ourselves, our neighbor, and the world, or it leads to disintegration. Life is driven by pangs of hunger—for love, health, beauty, truth, and wholeness. The trouble we run into is our misdiagnoses of the causes of hunger and our wrong ideas of what food will truly nourish and satisfy. Even if we are well-intentioned, we can look for rest in the wrong places.

This idea of hunger and fulfillment is so common in Christian circles that it almost becomes a cliché. And as with all clichés, so trite and commonplace at first glance, there is a deep mystery to satiation.

Saint Augustine points to this hunger as he begins his *Confessions*: "You have made us for yourself, and our heart is restless until it rests in you."[2] He goes on to describe our desires as being as many as the hairs on our heads rather than a single desire that unites us. Our desires go from pleasure to pleasure, disintegrating us, leading us away from ourselves and the God who made us for himself, leaving us in a perpetual state of restlessness.

Blaise Pascal describes our unrest as the God-shaped vacuum in the human heart that only Jesus can fill.[3] We can try to stuff it with things or pleasures or encounters or travel or experience, but none of these created things do the trick. Try as we might, we can't fill a Creator-sized vacuum with created things.

C. S. Lewis believes that in our search for rest our desire is not strong enough. He claims, "We are half-hearted creatures, fooling about with drink and sex and ambition when infinite joy is offered us, like an ignorant child who wants to go on making mud pies in a slum because he cannot imagine what is meant by the offer of a holiday

1. Rolheiser, *Holy Longing*, 5.
2. Augustine, *Confessions* 1.1.1 (Chadwick, 3).
3. Pascal, *Pensées*, 425.

at the sea. We are far too easily pleased."[4] God offers a luxurious vacation at an all-inclusive resort. But on the way, we get distracted with some mud that we imagine is more satisfying. God is cool, but a Tesla would be nice too.

These are the typical "worldly" pleasures that you may hear about in a sermon. But have you ever sought rest or fulfillment in the right places—or at least what others told you were right places—and found that they left you wanting? Have you read massive systematic theologies or spiritual formation books that had all the answers but discovered that they didn't cause the God-contentedness you sought? Have you practiced your daily personal devotions but found you did not seem to be growing closer to God? Have you tried being good, genuinely good, but ended up floundering and feeling like more of a failure? I've sought those kinds of rest too. These experiences may make us ask, *Am I the problem?*

THE GENESIS

This book began when a student critiqued a college class I teach on spiritual formation. Many people who have attended a college or university are familiar with the end-of-semester form: evaluate this class and this teacher. Typically, teachers can do two things with such feedback: ignore it or let it eat them alive. Praise can lead to pride, and the slightest criticism to despair. Naturally, I avoid them.

But sometimes I can't help myself. In one instance I looked and saw that a student complained about my class. Though the evaluation was anonymous, I had a pretty good idea who it was. The negative comments irked me, as they usually do. I had spent time with this particular student and knew the semester had been difficult, as they were struggling with personal issues. And after the time and effort I gave to this student, I was hurt to read their critique of a class that I had hoped would be an anchor in otherwise turbulent waters.

I desired the class to be experiential. What good is a class on spiritual formation if students aren't spiritually formed? And how does one nurture spiritual formation without *doing* something? So

4. Lewis, *Made for Heaven*, 26.

the class was oriented toward practice. We did in-class activities. I assigned devotional readings. We broke into accountability groups. We underwent self-evaluation.

But the student did not like the class—at all. Among other things, they found this particular class a waste of time and didn't learn anything. In fact, they wanted more lectures and less practice. To be clear, my goal in the classroom is for people to learn things and feel that their time and effort are well spent, so this critique stung a bit. And the feedback was surprising; since when did college students want *more* lectures?

But after some reflection, I decided this student was right. I did need to spend some time reflecting on the traditions behind the practices of formation. Doing the practices without understanding where they come from or how they fit together can still be formative. Taking inventory of our souls in the presence of another certainly won't hurt, even if we don't know the origin of the exercise. Likewise, meditation and prayer and Bible study will cultivate a deeper spirituality even in those who do not know the history of those practices. But knowing where they find their roots can deepen our appreciation for the whole of Christianity. This rootedness can provide stability when spirituality seems more like unrest than rest.

A RETRIEVAL PROJECT

My teaching brings me into contact with students who are at times in despair over the state of evangelical Christianity. Their frustrations are something I can relate to. I came to faith in a religious atmosphere that emphasized the new and the novel and rejected tradition. Traditional church structures were stale and dead. I felt like authorities or mentors were there to take advantage of me or manipulate me rather than to be stabilizing forces or to care for me. I had to make something of myself without trusting anyone or anything that came before me, and I had an obligation to define my own conception of happiness without reference to any other tradition or authority. This mentality left me with few resources to guide my life. I had shallow puddles but no deep wells. The shallowness of these resources was a problem, since defining happiness is a hard task. Depending on myself alone, I didn't have the resources to make wise decisions. I needed authority, tradition, and rules that would help me make sense of my place and myself. I was not as independent as I liked to imagine.

Some have blamed this push toward individualism and away from tradition as a by-product of the Reformation. One of the principles of the Reformation was *semper reformanda*: always be reforming. When I was first taught this phrase, it was explained as referring to each generation of the church needing a reformation because the church is prone to error. But the subtext I read into the phrase made me, the individual, the arbiter of correctness. For Protestants, it's easy to be a nontraditioned people. We're individuals, after all. The evangelical Christianity I knew seemed obsessed with the trendy at the expense of the traditional. The music was new and used hip styles. New pastors with fashionable clothing were in, while gray heads and suits were out. And priestly vestments weren't even considered. *We're not Catholic!*

But in myself and in the young people I teach, I have found a desire for roots and tradition. I remember trying to figure out something simple on my own: dating. Typically, this is an individual effort, a "beauty is in the eye of the beholder" sort of thing. Yet I remember being exasperated at the end of my dating trials and errors; most trials were indeed errors. I needed someone to tell me what to do, to give me some guidance. By the end, I knew enough not to trust myself.

The same was true in the church. I had seen people trying to re-invent Christianity, to make it more palatable and accessible. There were shallow reasons given for the practices in the church. I'd ask, "Why do we do it this way?" The response was, "Because it's the way we've done it"—for the past fifteen years, which was how long the church had been around. There was no biblical intentionality or historical precedence. There were no theological reasons. This was just the way the pastor did it. And I thought that there must be more to Christianity than this.

In the search for stability, I needed the "democracy of the dead," to use a phrase from the theologian G. K. Chesterton. Chesterton claims, "Tradition means giving votes to the most obscure of all classes, our ancestors. It is the democracy of the dead. Tradition refuses to submit to the small and arrogant oligarchy of those who merely happen to be walking about."[5] As I've begun my teaching career, I've seen what a ballast tradition can provide. If we look only to those walking about, we will be limited in our vision and action. I've found a great freedom in not having to reinvent the Christian faith.

Tradition, as it turns out, creates social continuity and personal density. Social continuity comes through the establishment of a language that is common to the past and the present day. This language connects past moments to the present moment in a way that makes actions and thoughts intelligible. Tradition gives us a language to speak and practices to inherit. Respecting those who have come before us is a way to respect those who come after us. It gives us guardrails so we don't swerve off the road.

Along with social continuity, tradition also provides personal density. "Personal density" refers to our ability to remain steadfast. Our culture is prone to live in the moment (#YOLO). Access to information is overwhelming, and trends change as quickly as the nightly news. Considering this reality, Alan Jacobs proposes that the greater one's understanding of the past is, the greater the personal density one has. He writes, "Personal density is directly proportional to 'temporal bandwidth,'" which Jacobs defines as "the width of your present, your *now*. . . . The more you dwell in the past and in the future, the thicker your bandwidth."[6] Personal density allows us not to be "tossed to and fro by the waves and carried about by every wind of doctrine, by human cunning, by craftiness in deceitful schemes" (Eph. 4:17), or by whatever the latest outrage on social media is. Tradition—knowledge of the past—brings a kind of stability and maturity in a shifting and changing world.

The Christianity in which I was formed seemed fifteen years old. But what about the two-thousand-year history of the church? Do we reject the first fifteen hundred years because "that's Catholic"? As a Protestant, do I have a tradition that is only five hundred years old? That's better, I guess, than fifteen years. But are there more ancient resources we can retrieve that deepen and enliven our lived Christianity?

5. Chesterton, *Orthodoxy*, 45.
6. Jacobs, *Breaking Bread with the Dead*, 19.

This book answers that last question in the affirmative. Our resources are deeper and richer than fifty years or five hundred years. We have two thousand years of church history that provide a social culture and density from which we can draw. This is the work of retrieval. Though I write as a Protestant, I explore different traditions and include exemplars beyond Protestant Christianity. I don't think Christianity began with the Reformation. I am gladly Protestant, but I also recognize that Catholic and Orthodox people and practices have something to teach us. They are our brothers and sisters, our fathers and mothers in the faith.

When I was growing up, a "quiet time" or devotional time in the morning was the most suggested practice for spiritual growth. That's about all I knew to do. A vibrant Christian has a quiet time. Quiet times can often seem like the silver bullet for all ailments. In sin? "Quiet time." Feeling anxious? "More personal devotions." Angry? "Get alone with God." To be sure, I am all for quiet time. I highly recommend it. But I also want to suggest other ways of formation beyond the standard solution. I want to introduce you to the rich history of Christian practices to give you more tools for your spiritual formation tool belt.

Students do not have to run to Buddhism to find resources for deep meditation and contemplative practices; Christianity has them. They don't need to run to communism to care about the poor; Christianity has the theological resources to love the lowly and the exemplars who have been faithful to that task. People don't need to join a bohemian commune to love the earth; there are deep ecological and environmental wells to draw from in Christianity. Those disenfranchised by the new and novel can go back to the ancient to find depth and breadth of Christian expression. Before we run to something else, we need to explore our own traditions.

INTRODUCING THE TRANSCENDENTALS

In classical philosophy, for anything to be real it must share some aspect of truth, goodness, and beauty. If something were completely evil, false, and ugly, it would not exist; it would be robbed of its substance, its realness. The term "transcendentals" points to the Transcendent One in which all things are made. For Plato, the

Transcendent was the world of perfect Forms. For the Christian, God is the perfect Form to which all things conform—the All-True, All-Good, and All-Beautiful, holding all three qualities in fullness and perfect unity. Part of what it means to be made in the image of God is to share these divine attributes of truth, goodness, beauty, and unity. Created beings have more or less of these aspects, but to exist at all is to share in the Transcendent. As such, no person is pure evil or pure ugliness. All things—from trees to birds to human beings—have semblances of truth, goodness, and beauty. And as the crown of creation, humanity images the Transcendent most closely and clearly.

The human powers to understand truth, goodness, and beauty correspond to our human nature: the mind, the will, and the heart. The mind knows the truth. The will chooses the good. The heart loves the beautiful. Traditionally, these qualities have been the core tenets of a liberal-arts curriculum: strengthening our human capacities to know, choose, and love by drawing on the best of human history. Part of being authentically human is growing in our capacities for truth, goodness, and beauty. We all hunger for these fundamental aspects of our being. To be real persons, substantive persons, it's necessary for us to develop our capacities in the transcendentals: to be more authentically true, more genuinely good, more compellingly beautiful, and more integrated people. *A Short Guide to Spiritual Formation* is a book about *being*. As such, my modest definition of spiritual formation is this: the process whereby the soul becomes more conformed to the image of God. The transcendentals are like food for our souls. Our modern world wants to fragment and segment us into bits and pieces that can be analyzed and mastered. I'm suggesting a way of formation that seeks to put us together and make us whole. Each transcendental is its own note, but together they form a single, unified major chord. Rather than being in competition, each transcendental plays in harmony with the others. If we recover truth, goodness, and beauty—along with community—our souls can be shaped into fuller being.

THE ROAD AHEAD

A Short Guide to Spiritual Formation is divided into four parts: truth, goodness, beauty, and community. Truth, goodness, and beauty broaden the soul's capacity for divine participation, and community deepens and integrates each in turn. Each transcendental provides a different stream or tradition of formation to channel our unrest. The transcendental streams aren't in competition but rather are more akin to tools in a tool belt. I want to provide a framework you can use in exploring richer and deeper traditions in case you ever become stagnant or think, *Is this all there is?*

Each part of the book will share certain commonalities. In structure, they each have three chapters. The first chapter will focus on the biblical precedents for the transcendental. The story of the Bible can be told in a way that highlights a certain transcendental, and the Lord's Supper showcases a distinctive of that transcendental. The second chapter is the historical, philosophical, and practical outworking of that stream of formation. My desire is for you to see that each transcendental not only has roots in Scripture but also has tradition that grounds it. The final chapter of each part features one exemplar from that stream. To riff on Saint Ambrose, God saves not by argument and reason but by lives.[7] We need to see what a life of faith looks like, so this last chapter presents a saint who enriches and enlivens the tradition discussed in that part of the book. We learn the Christian life through imitation and under the direction of a master. As Stanley Hauerwas posits, "The problem lies not in knowing *what* we must do, but *how* we are to do it. And the how is learned only by watching and following."[8] These exemplars show what a life of faithfulness looks like in different times and places—in persecution, in wealth and comfort, in slavery, in power, in poverty, in the marginalized status of a minority. The communion of saints helps us see ourselves as part of God's story as we watch and follow.

In his famous book *The Seven Storey Mountain*, Thomas Merton debates with himself about what he should be. A friend suggests that he should want to be a saint.[9] I think that's good advice. Saints take different forms. There's no single prescription for how sainthood

---

7. "But it was not by dialectic that it pleased God to save His people; 'for the kingdom of God consisteth in simplicity of faith, not in wordy contention'" (Ambrose, *On the Christian Faith* 1.5.42, in *Nicene and Post-Nicene Fathers*, 10:207).

8. Hauerwas, *Community of Character*, 131.

9. Merton, *Seven Storey Mountain*, 260.

happens or what it will look like. Defining goals too narrowly can be restrictive to a life of sainthood. The traditions of truth, goodness, beauty, and community lay out a broad life of holiness where we can find where we fit in.

Part 1 of this book highlights truth. The church is to "contend for the faith that was once for all delivered to the saints" (Jude 3). Faith is something heard and understood. Theology, thinking God's thoughts after him (in the words of Johannes Kepler), is an intellectual affair. From this theological foundation and a gospel centrality, good works flow. But if we get the gospel wrong, as Saint Paul shows in Galatians, then our whole foundation is flawed. Theology helps us stay grounded in the gospel. Saint Augustine, a fourth-century North African bishop, is the exemplar of truth, as he has a famous conversion story, and this conversion drove him to defend a pure faith with theological rigor.

Part 2 explores goodness. The Protestant temptation is to think that the pursuit of goodness leads to a works righteousness. However, living a life of virtue requires habits and rituals. God is concerned not just with our minds but also with our bodies and our lives. Part of being a Christian is growing in Christlikeness by bearing the fruits of the Spirit: putting off sin and putting on virtue. The exemplar is Dorothy Day, founder of the Catholic Worker movement of the twentieth century, whose work included caring for the homeless and destitute.

Part 3 focuses on beauty. While the goal of part 1 is to know God and the goal of part 2 is to be like Christ, the goal of the beauty tradition is to see God. In essence, we become what we behold, so we ought to seek the face of Jesus, in whose image we are being formed. Being detached from things that draw us away from God, we can attend to and contemplate his compelling beauty. Part 3 closes with a brief introduction to the life and work of the mystic Saint Teresa of Ávila, a sixteenth-century Spanish monastic.

Lest one think that spiritual formation is an individual affair, part 4 deepens the broad formation of the earlier parts by attending to community. I take the liberty of terming the transcendental of unity as "community," since Jesus prays for unity for the community that he establishes in his church (John 17). Whereas the previous three traditions emphasize the broadening of an individual person, community roots the individual in a place and among a people. This final part emphasizes the necessity of commitment to a local church and to stability in place. Because we are embodied individuals enmeshed in a web of relational and cosmic connections, part of the call of formation is nourishing the people and places that have nourished us. The German martyr Dietrich Bonhoeffer is utilized as the exemplar of communal commitment.

CONCLUSION

Jesus describes himself as the Good Shepherd. He proclaims that "I came that they may have life and have it abundantly" (John 10:10). The witness of the church is the witness to this life, this real, joyful, full life, a life most alive to life. We need the truth if we are to know God rightly and develop true affection for him. We need goodness if we are to develop a practical faith and intentional spirituality. We need beauty if we are to experience God on an intimate and deep level. We need relational bonds if we are to be known and loved. This book serves as an introduction to broadening and deepening our common faith.

We live in a world that is restless and discontented. We're not at home here, which is another way to say the same thing. Part of this restlessness is the human condition. We are always pilgrims, homeless and in search of a homeland. The spiritual writer Henri Nouwen points out that the search for rest presumes we have found or have access to truth, goodness, and beauty already. He asks, "How can I search for beauty or truth unless that beauty and truth are already known to me in the depth of my heart?"[10] Likewise, the band U2 sings a song called "I Still Haven't Found What I'm Looking For." I think many who listen to it relate to this longing. We know we're looking for something but are still searching and still have unrest about the fullness of this elusive thing.

The goodness of spirituality is that we do not have to find the transcendentals. The Transcendent has already found us.

10. Nouwen, *Life of the Beloved*, 44.

At the end of *The Giving Tree*, the children's book I mentioned earlier, the child comes back to that used-up tree. All the good gifts that the child abused are gone: no apples, no limbs, no trunk. The boy has sold the apples, built a house with the limbs, and used the trunk to build a boat to sail away in. All that remains is a stump. The last thing the tree has left to offer is a place to sit and rest.

As our hearts experience restlessness, God invites us to rest in him. We can use God's good gifts, but they are vanity unless we learn to rest. In this life, satiation will always be temporary. I wrote this book to help Christians find little stumps along the way of life. I pray *A Short Guide to Spiritual Formation* brings you a rest and stability that you've been yearning for.

PART I

TRUTH

THE THEOLOGICAL LIFE

OH Book! infinite sweetnesse! let my heart
    Suck ev'ry letter, and a hony gain,
    Precious for any grief in any part;
To cleare the breast, to mollifie all pain.

Thou art all health, health thriving till it make
    A full eternitie: thou art a masse
    Of strange delights, where we may wish & take.
Ladies, look here; this is the thankfull glasse,

That mends the lookers eyes: this is the well
    That washes what it shows. Who can indeare
    Thy praise too much? thou art heav'ns Lidger here,
Working against the states of death and hell.

    Thou art joyes handsell: heav'n lies flat in thee,
    Subject to ev'ry mounters bended knee.
            —George Herbert, "The Holy Scriptures I"

All Scripture is breathed out by God and profitable for teaching,
for reproof, for correction, and for training in righteousness, that
the man of God may be complete, equipped for every good work.
            —2 Timothy 3:16–17

1

The CENTRALITY of BIBLICAL TRUTH

GOD SPEAKS

> To a Christian man there can be nothing either more necessary or profitable, than the knowledge of holy Scripture, forasmuch as in it is contained God's true word, setting forth his glory, and also man's duty.
>
> —The Church of England's *First Book of Homilies*, Homily 1

Theology is important because God is important. But sometimes the God we believe in is not a God worthy of being believed. The God we imagine may not be the God of the Bible.

By and large, biblical literacy has gone down with each generation over the past one hundred years. The concern for a theological life is low. There's a stream of anti-intellectualism in evangelical Christianity that has been well documented.[1] As Mark Noll quips in his plea for evangelicals to take up the call of intellectual rigor, "The

1. See especially Noll, *Scandal of the Evangelical Mind*; Moreland, *Love Your God with All Your Mind*; Blamires, *The Christian Mind*; Guinness, *Fit Bodies, Fat Minds*.

scandal of the evangelical mind is that there is not much of an evan-gelical mind."[2] One seminary president summarizes the research of a recent Barna study:

> Fewer than half of all adults can name the four gospels. Many Chris-tians cannot identify more than two or three of the disciples. Accord-ing to data from the Barna Research Group, 60 percent of Americans can't name even five of the Ten Commandments. "No wonder people break the Ten Commandments all the time. They don't know what they are," said George Barna, president of the firm. The bottom line? "Increasingly, America is biblically illiterate."
>
> Multiple surveys reveal the problem in stark terms. According to 82 percent of Americans, "God helps those who help themselves," is a Bible verse. Those identified as born-again Christians did better—by one percent. A majority of adults think the Bible teaches that the most important purpose in life is taking care of one's family.
>
> Some of the statistics are enough to perplex even those aware of the problem. A Barna poll indicated that at least 12 percent of adults believe that Joan of Arc was Noah's wife. Another survey of gradu-ating high school seniors revealed that over 50 percent thought that Sodom and Gomorrah were husband and wife. A considerable number of respondents to one poll indicated that the Sermon on the Mount was preached by Billy Graham. We are in big trouble.[3]

How are we to believe in a God we do not really know? How are we to pass on a story that we don't know ourselves?

In 2005, when Christian Smith and his colleagues researched the re-ligious beliefs of teenagers, they found that the emerging generation—even those raised within the church—had some unorthodox beliefs. To summarize their findings, they coined the term "Moralistic Thera-peutic Deism." Essentially, this system of thought says there is a god who is largely indifferent and distant from people's lives (Deism) but who wants them to be good (moralistic) so that they feel better about themselves (therapeutic).[4] Earlier in the century, Richard Niebuhr

2. Noll, *Scandal of the Evangelical Mind*, 3.
3. Mohler, "Scandal of Biblical Illiteracy."
4. Officially, Moralistic Therapeutic Deism consists of five basic tenets: "1. A God exists who created and orders the world and watches over human life on earth. 2. God wants people to be good, nice, and fair to each other, as taught in the Bible

described a similar perversion of Christianity: "A God without wrath brought men without sin into a Kingdom without judgment through the ministrations of a Christ without a Cross."[5] In an effort to make Christianity more palatable to the modern generation, whole denominations were swept up into a false version of Christianity. Isn't a wrathful God outdated? Shouldn't we focus on human goodness rather than sin? Is our sin really so serious that it needs judgment? Isn't the cross a little gruesome for modern ears? ·

Sometimes the custom-made, curated God we profess is not worthy of being believed.

I write all this to document the state of theological literacy and doctrinal fidelity. There is not much to celebrate. In our culture and in the church, we seem to neglect truth. The problem is not just "out there"—how we are being deformed by culture. The problem is "in here"—how we as the church are catechizing young and old. For reasons known and unknown, those in the church are believing in a God that is not the one presented in the Scriptures. Without a doubt, a false view of God will affect how we are spiritually formed.

The weakening of truth claims in culture further complicates the church's public testimony. In order to avoid offense, we are prone to soft-pedal truth claims. As Americans, we believe in belief and the right to choose what to believe. We believe in a version of God that isn't interesting enough to warrant the attention involved in denial. Like Moralistic Therapeutic Deists, we've presented a bland God with no glory, a gospel with no need of judgment or forgiveness, a sanitized Jesus who issues no challenge to our otherwise comfortable lives. So, in the expression of Stanley Hauerwas, American Christianity has produced a people who say, without irony, "I believe Jesus is Lord—but that's just my personal opinion."[6] The inherent irony of such a statement is that "Jesus is Lord" cannot be relegated to personal opinion. The claim is a truth of cosmic reality. Whether you

---

and by most world religions. 3. The central goal of life is to be happy and to feel good about oneself. 4. God does not need to be particularly involved in one's life except when God is needed to resolve a problem. 5. Good people go to heaven when they die" (C. Smith and Denton, *Soul Searching*, 162–63).

5. Niebuhr, *Kingdom of God in America*, 193.

6. Hauerwas, "End of American Protestantism."

believe it or not, Jesus is Lord. The lordship of Christ is not a matter of "personal opinion."

We all believe something. The goal of theology or truth-seeking is to believe God as he is rather than how we want him to be. That's a difficult task because we're all prone to imagine God in our own image—as someone who likes what we like, who has the same enemies we have, and so on.

False doctrine is like a smudge of dirt on a window, obscuring God's being and attributes. The resulting corrupted picture of God has an impact on our own development. As Ellen Charry notes, "By and large, whether intentionally or inadvertently, willingly or unwillingly, reflectively or innocently, we become what we know."[7] Likewise, we cannot become what we do not know. Our knowing is our becoming.

THE STORY OF TRUTH IN THE BIBLE

Living in accordance with the truth is central to the Bible. In the beginning, God spoke, and what God said was intelligible. God communicates and condescends to human understanding. What a profound and unique reality of Christianity! God wants to be known, so he uses language and concepts that humans can understand.

Early in our origin story, a slithering snake sneaks into the great garden that God creates. He asks the woman a simple question: "Did God actually say . . . ?" (Gen. 3:1). All of a sudden, deception creeps into the human imagination. Maybe God didn't tell Adam and Eve the truth. Maybe the serpent is more trustworthy. The temptation to "be like God, knowing good and evil" (3:5) is too much to bear. The woman sees that the tree "was to be desired to make one wise" (3:6), so she takes the fruit and eats it. Our first parents thought wisdom came through satanic schemes and that they were sufficient apart from God to discern where truth was found.

The story of Israel is a story of promise and the failure to remember. God makes covenants with his people, leads them out of bondage "with an outstretched arm" (e.g., Exod. 6:6), and rescues them over

7. Charry, By the Renewing of Your Minds, 26.

and over—and the people of Israel forget. Psalm 78 recounts much of the Jewish narrative this way. The psalmist pleads with his readers to "give ear . . . to my teaching" (v. 1) and "tell to the coming generation the glorious deeds of the LORD, and his might, and the wonders that he has done" (v. 4). Remembering the teaching and glorious deeds of God was the way the people of Israel catechized their young. But as the psalmist goes through Israel's history, we learn that they kept forgetting. The story of Israel could be told as God continuing to show mercy and the people of Israel regularly forgetting what God has done. (And the story of the church isn't much different, unfortunately!) Israel cannot dodge the blame. The burden of passing on the words and works of God faithfully falls on the elder generations.

The cycles of forgetfulness end with the coming of Jesus. Jesus is the God-man who remembers. Like our first parents in the garden and like Israel in the wilderness, Jesus is tempted by the devil so what is in his heart can be seen (Matt. 4:1; see Deut. 8:2). At every turn, Jesus invokes the true wisdom of God in response to the false wisdom of Satan. The memorized words of God in Scripture are the means by which Jesus counteracts the lies he hears from the tempter. And in facing the devil in this way, he succeeds where Adam and Eve failed. He remembers what Israel forgot.

We are invited into the same victory through remembrance. One thing we all must remember is our baptism. The Father's words to Jesus at his baptism are also God's words to us as we are found in him: "This is my beloved [child], with whom I am well pleased" (Matt. 3:17). All Christian maturity finds its root in being a beloved child of God. When we forget that, when we work *for* our salvation rather than *from* our salvation, things go haywire. More broadly, we must also engage in the continual hearing of the Word of God. "Faith comes from hearing," the apostle Paul says (Rom. 10:17). And this is not a onetime hearing; Paul writes to the Corinthian church to remind them of the gospel they have already heard and received (1 Cor. 15:1). Biblical truths need repeating because we are prone to forget. When we hear the Word repeatedly and remember it, we can be "transformed by the renewal of [our] mind[s], that by testing [we] may discern what is the will of God" (Rom. 12:2). On Romans 12, Charry comments, "For Paul, mental transformation required

7

for excellent living derives from the Greek observation that knowing goodness precedes being good."[8] That's why Paul directs church leaders to preach the Word (2 Tim. 4:2) and "insist on these things" (Titus 3:8): from the truth flow good works.

God creates in truth. Humanity falls by the deception of lies. We continue to forget the truth. Jesus comes to us embodying the truth in himself. The church is founded on the truth of Christ and instructs Jesus's disciples by telling the gospel story over and over again, every week. A key to salvation history is remembering that salvation history. To remember the truth presumes we know it already. But because we forget, we need to be reminded. Rightly remembering leads to obedience.

THE SUPREMACY OF THE WORD OF GOD

Here is the truth: God speaks. And when God speaks, things happen. Pay attention.

Truth is embedded in the cosmic story and even in the way the Hebrew Scriptures (meaning the Old Testament books) are put together. When Jesus refers to the Hebrew Scriptures, he calls them "the Law and the Prophets" or "Moses and the Prophets" (Matt. 5:17; Luke 24:27). This Hebrew grouping of books is different from the grouping of books in most Protestant Old Testaments. The grouping called the Law (or Pentateuch) is the same: Genesis through Deuteronomy. The Prophets section includes Joshua through Kings (according to the Protestant order) as well as what Christians know as the prophetic books, except for Daniel. The Writings grouping has everything else: the Wisdom books (Job through Song of Songs), Lamentations, Daniel, Ruth, Esther, Ezra–Nehemiah, and Chronicles. The order of the books within these groupings was not fixed in the beginning, when the books were first completed, but it is nevertheless enlightening to consider the books that were eventually, in the tradition of Judaism, placed first in each of the groupings.

The first book of the Law, in the Hebrew order as in the Protestant order, is Genesis. In Genesis 1, God creates the universe from

8. Charry, *By the Renewing of Your Minds*, 4.

nothing. He speaks words into the void, and creation starts emerging. From the divine mind, words go forth. By his speech he forms the formless space: day and night, waters above and waters below, land and water (days 1–3). And then, by his Word, he fills the space he has formed: sun and moon in the heavens, birds in the sky, fish in the water, animals on the land (days 4–6). He forms and fills the formless and empty space. His speech holds creative power. Then God gives the first humans commands to remember for their flourishing (Gen. 1:22; 2:16–17). If they rightly remember, they will reside in peace and joy and life. But as we have seen, things go haywire.

The Prophets section begins with Joshua. In this book there's a great transition. Moses will not lead the people into the promised land. Joshua steps into the leadership void, and Moses instructs Joshua this way: "Be strong and courageous. Do not be frightened, and do not be dismayed, for the LORD your God is with you wherever you go" (Josh. 1:9). But before that, Moses says, "This Book of the Law shall not depart from your mouth, but you shall meditate on it day and night, so that you may be careful to do according to all that is written in it. For then you will make your way prosperous, and then you will have good success" (1:8). At a great turning point in salvation history, the mantle of leadership requires devotion and meditation on the Word of God. Success hinges on meditation. Don't forget these words.

The next major division of the Hebrew Bible, the Writings, begins with the Psalms. Psalm 1 outlines the way to blessing: meditation on the law day and night (v. 2). The one who meditates on the law "is like a tree planted by streams of water that yields its fruit in its season, and its leaf does not wither" (v. 3). The words of God are life-giving and soul-sustaining. Remember that. Meditate on the words. Know them. Don't forget them.

The Psalms consistently appeal to the goodness of the law, statutes, testimonies, and words of God. The longest of the Psalms, 119, is a poem meditating on, treasuring, appreciating, and loving the commands and the words of God. It is an acrostic poem in which every letter of the Hebrew alphabet begins a stanza. So, the first line of verses 1–8 start with *aleph* (the Hebrew *a*), and the first line of verses 9–16 start with *bet* (the Hebrew *b*). One really has to love the commandments of God to write a poem with 176 verses and that much intentionality! But the psalmist wants us to take time and see that the law of God is worth meditating on day and night. Don't forget the truths of God.

Psalm 19 extols the law of God as being "perfect," "sure," "right," "pure," "clean," and "true" (vv. 7–9). The testimony of the Lord revives the soul, makes the simple wise, rejoices the heart, enlightens the eyes, and endures forever. Who doesn't want that? The commandments of God are more precious than gold and sweeter than honey. In Ezekiel 3, when the prophet is told to eat the scroll, he describes the words of God in the same way: "It was in my mouth as sweet as honey" (Ezek. 3:3). Not only are the words from God true, but they are a treat.

The rest of the Old Testament testifies to the goodness, power, and wisdom of the words from God. Later, Ezekiel is taken to a valley of dry bones—"very dry" bones, as the text says (Ezek. 37:2). These bones have been there a long time. God asks, "Can these bones live?" and Ezekiel says, "O Lord God, you know" (v. 3). Then God tells Ezekiel to prophesy to these dry bones, telling them they will live. As the prophet obeys, he hears the valley start rattling. These bones, which have been dead a long time, come together, and sinews and flesh form on them. God's Word creates, as we saw in Genesis 1. God's prophetic speech also makes dead things come alive.

Nehemiah is a book about rebuilding the ruins of Jerusalem after the Babylonian exile. Over and over throughout the Old Testament, God comes to rescue his people as he gently prods them toward repentance. But after the people ignore and forget God long enough, the consequence is serious, though not permanent: the land that God gave to the Israelites—so they could steward it, bring *shalom* as in the garden, and be a "light for the nations" (Isa. 49:6) and a kingdom of priests and a holy nation (Exod. 19:6)—is taken over, and the Israelites are carried off to Babylon.

Years later, Nehemiah is sent on a task to return to the land of promise, rebuild the walls of Jerusalem, and rebuild the people of God in the place of God. During their exile, foreign countries came and destroyed their city and temple. All that they held dear has been left in ruins. Under the leadership of Nehemiah, exiled Israel makes plans for, and executes, the rebuilding of the walls to protect God's chosen city—the city of peace, Jeru-*shalom*. But the city's physical protection is not the biggest concern for Israel. The walls are a sign not of seclusion from invaders but of their identity as a distinct people. The distinction of Israel is that they have God's revelation, the revelation of the one true God.

In the law of Moses, when he predicts the people will enter the land and establish a monarchy, Moses gives instructions on what the king should be like and what he should do. The king is required to copy the law of God—all of it—and read it every day. Why? "That he may learn to fear the LORD his God by keeping all the words of this law and these statutes" (Deut. 17:19). It's not clear that any king practiced this requirement, yet I wonder how the history of Israel would have been different if their leaders had remembered the law.

So, with the king's role in mind, Nehemiah and his compadres build an elevated platform. And they bring before the people the precious, long-forgotten book—the law of Moses, this text that the psalmist says is sweeter than honey and more to be desired than gold (Ps. 19:10)—and the scribe Ezra starts reading. He reads for six hours (Neh. 8:1–8). (And you think it's hard to sit through a forty-five-minute sermon!)

Having been deprived of the life-giving, soul-stirring, resurrecting power of the Word of God, these former exiles long for what God has spoken. The text says the people's ears are attentive (Neh. 8:3). They are leaning in, expectant, eager to hear God's Word. They shout, "Amen, Amen" (v. 6). They bow their faces to the ground in worship. The people of Israel have neglected what God said to pay attention to and have forgotten his words. But now the Word of God becomes central to this city rebuilt out of ruins.

The biblical story pauses after the rebuilding of the renewed Jerusalem. The people remember God's written Word, but now his voice seems lost and distant.

And then, hundreds of years later, the Word of God becomes flesh and dwells among them (John 1:14). The spoken word of Genesis 1 becomes an embodied Word in the person of Jesus.

After Jesus is anointed in his baptism and defeats the temptations of Satan in the wilderness, he begins his ministry. And he begins his ministry by teaching. He goes to his local synagogue and takes a scroll—the Word of God that is to be with the people of God—and he reads. God speaks, Moses documents, the king copies, Ezekiel prophesies, and Nehemiah reads. Now Jesus takes his place and speaks the recorded Word of God:

> The Spirit of the Lord is upon me,
>> because he has anointed me
>> to proclaim good news to the poor.
> He has sent me to proclaim liberty to the captives
>> and recovering of sight to the blind,
>> to set at liberty those who are oppressed,
> to proclaim the year of the Lord's favor. (Luke 4:18–19; see
>> Isa. 61:1–2)

Jesus rolls the scroll back up. He sits down, and he says, "Today this Scripture has been fulfilled" (Luke 4:21). Whereas the previous prophets read or prophesied or spoke or meditated, Jesus comes on the scene and incarnates the words of Scripture. These are not abstract ideas or tidbits of information that are true. Jesus comes and embodies those words. He is them. Jesus says, in effect, "Today, God comes to you with good news of himself and liberty to the captives." When God speaks, he continues to embody his words with the same creative and resurrecting power we saw in the Old Testament. But the words have become a person. The Word becomes flesh and dwells among us. To borrow a term from the hip-hop artist Paul Wall, Christianity is "trill": true and real.

The early church is sent to witness to the "trill" salvific acts of God in Jesus Christ: to teach all nations everything that Jesus has commanded (Matt. 28:18–20). The early Christians devote themselves to the apostles' teaching (Acts 2:42), among other things. When Philip goes to a desert place, he crosses paths with an Ethiopian eunuch returning from a visit to Jerusalem (Acts 8). The eunuch is reading Isaiah 53 but confesses that he can't understand it unless someone explains it. If Philip can't get from Isaiah 53 to the gospel, then there's a problem. Philip tells him about the sacrifice of Jesus, which saves people from sin and punishment. Part of the ecclesial task is to explain the Scriptures, to teach the truth, to remind people of the Word of God.

Truth's climax is not in mere intellectual understanding but in affectional praise and wonder. Romans 1–11 is perhaps the richest theological text of all time. In it, Paul deals with sin, justification, salvation, promises made, promises kept, struggles with sin, guilt and condemnation, freedom, and hope. And after all that theology, he ends like this:

> Oh, the depth of the riches and wisdom and knowledge of God! How unsearchable are his judgments and how inscrutable his ways!
>
> > "For who has known the mind of the Lord,
> >   or who has been his counselor?"
> > "Or who has given a gift to him
> >   that he might be repaid?"
>
> For from him and through him and to him are all things. To him be glory forever. Amen. (Rom. 11:33–36)

Theology leads to doxology. The point of knowing the truth is not to feel superior or to answer skeptics. The point of meditating on the law day and night is to know and love the God who gave us the words.

REMEMBERING THE LORD'S SUPPER

In the truth tradition, we can see the Lord's Supper as a continual reminder. We are prone to forget, and Jesus invites us into a continual reminder. Jesus instructs, "Do this in remembrance of me" (Luke 22:19). To remember is a mental act. Remember your sin, which nailed Jesus to the cross. Remember the suffering Jesus endured. Remember the forgiveness that flows from the cross. Remember how Jesus loved you. Remember salvation. Remember that this meal is a foretaste of the marriage supper of the Lamb at the end of the ages. Remember the gospel. Don't forget it.

Active knowledge like this was often the way Israel passed on its faith to its children. The people were instructed in a ritual, and the expectation was that children would ask, "Why are we doing this?" (see Exod. 31:13; Lev. 23:43). Then Israel's elders were to tell them. To take but one example, consider the memorial stones set up by Joshua after they crossed the Jordan into the promised land. These stones were meant to be a sign to their children. "When your children ask in time to come, 'What do those stones mean to you?' then you shall tell them that the waters of the Jordan were cut off before the ark of the covenant of the LORD. When it passed over the Jordan, the waters of the Jordan were cut off. So these stones shall be to the people of Israel a memorial forever" (Josh. 4:6–7). Through this event, the people of Israel arrived at an understanding that they could not have reached any other way.

The Lord's Supper functions with a similar dynamic. It's only by participation that we can more fully know the Jesus behind the material elements. It seems as though Jesus often reveals himself through meals. On the road to Emmaus he interprets Old Testament passages through the life of the Messiah. The two disciples don't know who Jesus is until he breaks bread. This moment creates a great ritual realization. Eating leads to seeing. In the Eucharist, Christ doesn't teach by mere words. He gives us something we can taste, touch, and see. The Word doesn't stay as Word but becomes flesh. He meets his embodied people with his body.

From this we can tell that remembering is a mental act but also something more than that. Remembering the details of Jesus's life and death are also ways of abiding in his life and death (John 6:53–56). Remembering takes us back to visceral reactions and deep emotions. If you were to remember the best moment of your life, I'm sure your heart would beat a bit faster and a grin would emerge on your face. There's something about remembering that takes us back and produces bodily reactions. Likewise, if I were to ask you to remember the worst moment of your life, I'm sure you could feel the shame or terror of that moment as if it were happening right then. Remembering is an embodied and holistic action that re-members, puts things together, reconciles. Remembering Christ in the Eucharist is a kind of return in which Christ can heal us. Christ invites us to take himself into our very being, where he can put together the pieces that are broken and fragmented. To remember is to realize and recall that who I am is a process and a story in which God is with me during every act. By remembering, we invite God in to heal our broken memories.

Real remembering, deep remembering, is a kind of return: a return to the cross, a return to forgiveness, a return to Eden, a return to God. If we do the hard work of rightly remembering, there we encounter a healing truth.

Truth matters because the gospel matters. "Gospel" means "good news," and the news needs to be true for it to be good. The premise of this book is that all spiritual formation finds its roots in the gospel of grace. This gospel must be known, stewarded, heralded, and, in the Lord's Supper, remembered.

Martin Luther explains what gospel ministry is all about when he writes,

> Here I must take counsel of the gospel. I must hearken to the gospel, which teacheth me, not what I ought to do, (for that is the proper office of the law,) but what Jesus Christ the Son of God hath done for me: to wit, that He suffered and died to deliver me from sin and death. The gospel willeth me to receive this, and to believe it. And this is the truth of the gospel. It is also the principal article of all Christian doctrine, wherein the knowledge of all godliness consisteth.
>
> Most necessary it is, therefore, that we should know this article well, teach it unto others, and beat it into their heads continually.[9]

Knowing the gospel, teaching it to others, and "beat[ing] it into their heads continually"—this is what the truth tradition values. We need it. One way to define Christian ministry is as a regular reminder. We're prone to forget, but spiritual formation is grounded in remembering the goodness of the gospel of God.

---

9. Luther, *Commentary on St. Paul's Epistle to the Galatians*, 206.

✳ **2** ✳

The STORY-SHAPED LIFE

FROM A DEVOTIONAL FAITH TO A DEEP FAITH

Sanctify them in the truth; your word is truth.

—John 17:17

What are we to do? The question seems simple and innocent enough, but it's actually complex. In his book *After Virtue*, the philosopher Alasdair MacIntyre claims, "I can only answer the question 'What am I to do?' if I can answer the prior question 'Of what story or stories do I find myself a part?'"[1] He notices that the stories we tell give shape and meaning to our lives. We live a narrative life. It's an undeniable part of morality: we can say what's good only when we understand what story we are in. Stories provide the good or goal that we are to pursue.

1. MacIntyre, *After Virtue*, 216.

Let me explain by drawing attention to a false story we tell our-selves. Stanley Hauerwas argues that the project of modernity is an "attempt to produce a people who believe that *they should have no story except the story that they choose when they had no story*."[2] I think Hauerwas's description of modernity is probably the narra-tive that feels most natural. We don't choose a story—nay, we ought not choose a story—until we consciously opt in. We are part of no story by default, and we have endless stories to choose from. We are individuals, and we are free. The presumption of this story is that I get to make up my own life. So when someone asks, "What am I to do?" the answer is, "Whatever you want to do." No one can tell us what to do. There is no good for our lives that can be scripted. We are making it up.

But the story of not having a story is still a story. It's like a man thinking he has freedom to buy whatever he wants in a grocery store. In a sense, that's true. But he is limited to the options in the grocery store, and those choices were made before he got there. We're not as free to choose as we think we are. We've inherited the story even if we didn't choose it.

In literature, a tragedy is defined as a serious story where all rela-tionships function in a power struggle. There is no happy ending. It's a dog-eat-dog world out there, and we need to be mature and look at the grim reality in the face. You were born. You will die. Find mean-ing between point A (birth) and point B (death), but meaning and purpose will not outlast you. Depend on no one. Trust no authority or tradition. You only live once, so make choices that make you happy.

But what if we don't live in a tragedy? What if it's not up to us to find meaning, purpose, and pleasure? What if the true story is more of a comedy and less of a tragedy?

In literature, a comedy is not necessarily a funny story, if by "funny" we mean that it makes people laugh. A comedy is a story with a happy ending. The narrative may contain sadness, but we find reasons for hope even amid trials and suffering. It's a different story than the modern one that we have no story until we choose a story. In this comedy, none of us is the main character in the story after all.

2. Hauerwas, "End of American Protestantism" (emphasis added).

At best, we pass by as extras. In this Christian story, we don't have to fight to discover or find love. Love finds us.

And if love finds us, then we are not heroes raging against the competition of the world like characters in a tragedy; we are ordinary people, connecting with one another and all creation through the love that inspired the stars. This story causes us to give a different answer to the question, "What am I to do?" It lays out a different vision of the good life.

In order to live well, people need to be shaped by a true story. In another context, Hauerwas writes, "No society can be just or good that is built on falsehood. The first task of Christian social ethics, therefore, is not to make the 'world' better or more just, but to help Christian people form their community consistent with their conviction that the story of Christ is a truthful account of our existence."[3] The purpose of this chapter is to sketch that true story of Christ and show how this truthful account of our existence narrates the way we live and what we are to do.

THE FRAMING NARRATIVE

I love the way Dorothy Sayers connects doctrine (dogma) and story (drama). She says,

> Official Christianity, of late years, has been having what is known as bad press. We are constantly assured that the churches are empty because preachers insist too much upon doctrine—dull dogma as people call it. The fact is the precise opposite. It is the neglect of dogma that makes for dullness. The Christian faith is the most exciting drama that ever staggered the imagination of man—and the dogma is the drama.[4]

Along the same lines, C. S. Lewis calls Christianity the "true myth": it's the orienting story in which all other stories find their purpose and fulfillment.[5] We love rising tension and battles between good

---

3. Hauerwas, *Community of Character*, 10.
4. Sayers, *Letters to a Diminished Church*, 1.
5. C. S. Lewis writes, "Now the story of Christ is simply a true myth: a myth working on us the same way as the others, but with this tremendous difference that it

and evil. We all have a desire to be redeemed and healed by an act of sacrificial love. There's something primal about these paradigmatic stories. Lewis argues that all good stories reflect the ultimate story: Jesus Christ conquering sin by laying down his life in love. All lasting and meaningful stories are modeled after that first "myth." The problem is not preaching or dogma or assertions of truth. Dogma is not cold and stale. Dogma is the life-giving force of the universe. When the church retreats from the dogma contained in the drama, it's no wonder the world is uninterested in what we have to say.

Sayers continues,

> It is the dogma that is the drama—not beautiful phrases, nor comforting sentiments, nor vague aspirations to loving-kindness and uplift, nor the promise of something nice after death—but the terrifying assertion that the same God who made the world, lived in the world and passed through the grave and gate of death. Show that to the heathen, and they may not believe it; but at least they may realize that here is something that a man might be glad to believe.[6]

The Christian story is the most beautiful, compelling, rich story in the world. Our dogma is anything but boring or irrelevant.

It all started with God creating "all things visible and invisible," as the Nicene Creed says. The pinks of the sky at sunset and the taste combination of carne asada tacos both have their origin in the good God of the universe. God creates all things for the purpose of returning praise to himself by our enjoying what he created. He made a cosmic playground for us to enjoy, and he invites us to participate in pushing back the chaos and ugliness of the world and to join him in spreading order and beauty and peace. The sense deep in our hearts that we were made for adventure turns out to be true: God invites us to participate with him in the redemption of the world.

Yet rather than live under the good care of our Creator, we try to be our own gods. We listened to the devious voice of the serpent rather than the gracious voice of God. I don't think I need to explain this

---

really happened: and one must be content to accept it in the same way, remembering that it is God's myth where the others are men's myths" (Lewis, *Collected Letters of C. S. Lewis*, 1:997).

6. Sayers, *Letters to a Diminished Church*, 20.

part of the story very much. We all know that something is fundamentally wrong. Things are not the way they are supposed to be. Children are trafficked. Workers are exploited. People are homeless. We feel isolated and disconnected from others. Our closest relationships—those with family members, spouses, friends—are sometimes racked with conflict and anger. And I haven't even begun to mention the conflict within our souls. The guilt we carry and the shame that burdens us feel unbearable at times. We don't feel at peace in our own skin. We don't do what we want to do, and the things we know we should do seem impossible (see Rom. 7:15–20). No matter how hard we try to change, no matter the methods we use or the people we ask for help, it feels like we'll always be helpless and hopeless. Who can save us when our main problem is ourselves?

Well, "thanks be to God through Jesus Christ" (Rom. 7:25) that he did not leave us helpless. Christ came down to us, and the Maker was made in the womb of a virgin. The independent became dependent. God got breastfed. He entered the world to take the human plight of sin upon himself. The Creator God came to his own creation to be rejected and killed by his own people. The hands that God made slapped him. The mouths that God formed spat upon him. "But God shows his love for us in that while we were still sinners, Christ died for us" (Rom. 5:8). We didn't clean ourselves up. We didn't turn our lives around. Even while we were sinners, in the depths of despair, at our very worst, Christ died for us. He was raised from the dead because he never sinned, so death had no power over him. He then ascended into heaven, and now he sits at the right hand of the Father, whence he will come again to judge the living and the dead. When Jesus returns, there will no longer be pain or suffering or cancer or injustice. God will put all wrongs right. "He will wipe away every tear from [our] eyes" (Rev. 21:4).

Before he returns, God is forming a new community in which we are accepted not on the basis of our performance or social status or family background but on the basis of our faith in this Christ who came for us. The beloved community reaches out in love to a dying and broken world, seeking to mend and heal, to take on wounds and bind them up in Christ. This new people is founded on the cross, where guilt is washed away and shame is banished. Since it was founded in grace, there's no measuring up or jockeying for social position; rather, we are free in love to serve one another beyond natural boundaries and personal preferences.

This is our story, and it frames the answer to the question, "What are we to do?" The doctrines are the drama. And the drama becomes richer and fuller as we understand more dogma, as we read the Bible, study the creeds, know church history. Sayers is right. People may not believe this story. That's fair. But they would be glad to; they should hope this story is true. You may or may not discern whether the narrative is true, but it's anything but boring. The dogma is the drama.

THE TRUTH WILL SET YOU FREE

Since the gospel is the truth to be remembered and heard, it's necessary that we get the gospel right. The apostle Paul is certainly concerned with the gospel of grace. In Galatians he chastises the Judaizers who have tried to add requirements to the free gift of grace. Galatians is Paul's most hostile letter, because if we get the gospel wrong, we get our lives wrong. The truth is a matter of life and death. What we believe determines how we live.

A bishop in the Anglican church, C. FitzSimons Allison, argues in his book *The Cruelty of Heresy* that heresy is not simply something that gets the facts wrong. Heresy contains seeds that grow into cruelty. False teaching has victims, and the worse the teaching, the worse the cruelty that results. Souls are hanging in the balance based on the truths we communicate as Christians. Truth is not merely a beneficial tool to help people cope with the demands of life. Orthodox theologian Alexander Schmemann develops this dynamic further when he writes, "For Christianity, help is not the criterion. Truth is the criterion. The purpose of Christianity is not to help people by reconciling them with death but to reveal the Truth about life and death in order that people may be saved by this Truth."[7] The question is not, first, "Does this help or not?" Rather, the question is, "Is it true?" Salvation is at stake. The intensity of our belief or

7. Schmemann, *For the Life of the World*, 120.

the authenticity of our conduct is not the standard; biblical truth is the standard.

In 1 Corinthians the apostle Paul writes to remind the Corinthian church of the gospel "which you received, in which you stand, and by which you are being saved" (1 Cor. 15:1–2). The gospel is not something we graduate from as we move on to mature things like eschatology (the study of the last things). No, the gospel is for all of life. It's something that we "received" (past tense), "in which [we] stand" (present tense), and "by which [we] are being saved" (present continuous tense). To the apostle Paul, this reminding is "of first importance" (15:3). In other words, Paul is saying that justification by grace through faith is not only a necessary step in salvation but is the basis of sanctification. As Jonathan Dodson contends, "To be gospel-centered is not only to believe the gospel for salvation but to continually return to it for transformation."[8] The Reformation maintained this important emphasis: having begun by faith, the Christian continues on by faith (cf. Gal. 3:3). We do not get saved by faith and then grow in maturity by works. Faith is the basis, and grace is the motivation, of all spiritual growth. When the doctrines of personal sin and free forgiveness take root in the human soul, transformation happens. These truths must go deeper than intellectual comprehension. They must be known and experienced.

In Richard Lovelace's important work *Renewal as a Way of Life*, he examines great revivals of history, from the Reformation to the First Great Awakening, and notes shared elements. From this study he derives the preconditions of renewal, the primary elements of renewal, and the secondary elements of renewal. The preconditions of renewal are an awareness of God's holiness and an awareness of the depth of sin. In the theological imagination, one leads to the other. We cannot know God without knowing our sinfulness. And knowing ourselves means knowing our limits. As John Calvin contends in his *Institutes of the Christian Religion*, "The infinitude of good which resides in God becomes more apparent from our poverty. . . . Thus, our feeling of ignorance, vanity, want, weakness, in short, depravity and corruption, reminds us that in the Lord, and none but he,

---

8. Dodson, *Gospel-Centered Discipleship*, 13.

dwell the true light of wisdom, solid virtue, exuberant goodness."[9] Coming to the end of ourselves and our own efforts leads us into the arms of God.

Isaiah 6 provides a fitting biblical example. King Uzziah, a long-lasting and well-loved king, has died, and his death has left a huge void for the people of Israel. Isaiah is given a vision of the throne room of God: it is full of smoke, the train of God's robe filling the temple, the pillars quaking, the seraphim singing. The prophet has a vision of the true King who sits on the throne, and it's mysteriously terrifying.[10] In light of God's holiness, Isaiah sees his own and his people's sinfulness. "Woe is me! For I am lost; for I am a man of unclean lips, and I dwell in the midst of a people of unclean lips; for my eyes have seen the King, the LORD of hosts!" (Isa. 6:5). A recognition of God's holiness and our sin is the precondition for revival.

These realizations result in the primary elements of renewal—namely, justification, sanctification, the indwelling of the Holy Spirit, and authority in spiritual conflict. All of these are found in union with Christ. God's holiness and our sinfulness need to be resolved. Like Isaiah, we need our lips to be cleansed (Isa. 6:6–7). Justification is the truth that Martin Luther rediscovered in the Reformation: there is nothing we can do to earn God's favor, but it is given freely as a gift through faith. "For our sake he made him to be sin who knew no sin, so that in him we might become the righteousness of God" (2 Cor. 5:21). Justification necessarily leads to our sanctification, as we desire to obey this God who has saved us. The Holy Spirit testifies that we are children of God and cries out to him from within our hearts, saying, "Abba! Father!" (Gal. 4:6; Rom. 8:16; cf. 8:15). Through sanctification we experience greater success in our conflict with sin and see more fruit in our effort in pursuing righteousness. As gospel truths begin to take residence in our hearts, we move from selfish enjoyment to sacrificial love of one another. We turn from our egotistical pleasures and go out into the world, seeking to bring ultimate joy in God to our neighbors. This shift brings us to the secondary elements of renewal: mission, prayer, community, and theological

---

9. Calvin, *Institutes of the Christian Religion* 1.1.1. (Beveridge, 4).

10. For a further study of the tremendous mystery at the heart of religious experience, see Otto, *Idea of the Holy*, 12–41.

integration. We act out of our understanding of God's grace, which comes to us in the gospel.

Formation in truth works like this: when we hear the truth, a reality comes to reside deep in our souls, and that truth, as it drives deeper and deeper, causes us to externalize our internal realizations. As the gospel goes deep, our hearts open up to others. And when the gospel reaches our inmost being, we split open to see the needs of our neighbors. The start of this process is a simple acknowledgment of the truth: I am a great sinner, and Christ is a great Savior.

THE IMPORTANCE OF TRUE PREACHING

Martin Luther knew what it was like to doubt. Formed in medieval Catholicism, he never knew whether he was good enough. Sure, perhaps his sins were forgiven, but when would he be accepted? How much did he have to do? How often did he have to confess? What if he forgot to confess certain sins? He drove himself crazy.

In one of these moments of madness, he read the Epistle to the Romans and, with a deeper sense than ever before, saw that "the righteousness of God is a gift of God by which a righteous man lives, namely faith, and that sentence: The righteousness of God is revealed in the Gospel, is passive, indicating that the merciful God justifies us by faith, as it is written: 'The righteous shall live by faith.'"[11] To Luther, it was as if he had entered paradise. He was already accepted by God through faith. He didn't need to perform or work for his acceptance. His conscience could rest in the grace of Christ by belief.

Luther did not have a problem of doing. He had a problem of knowing. What he needed was a deeper realization of a truth hidden or otherwise unknown. The gospel had to sink in, and in order for that to happen, Luther needed the external Word to do its work. He needed the faith that comes by hearing (Rom. 10:17). He needed a revival of truth.

Martin Luther set out to reform the Catholic Church based on his understanding of justification by grace. Famously, he nailed his Ninety-Five Theses to the Wittenberg church door and began

11. Oberman, *Luther*, 184.

lecturing in the university. Foundational to the Reformation was seeking the truth.[12] In the aftermath of the Protestant Reformation, the reforming did not end with what the church believed. Reform meant changing the liturgy and the architecture of the church. The traditional liturgy had two parts: the ministry of the Word and the ministry of the sacrament. The table or altar stood in the center of the front of the church because in the Roman Catholic Church the sacraments were seen as the most important part of formation. In some Reformed churches, the sermon became the central element of a worship service, and the pulpit became the central feature of the space. This shift meant that God was to be heard more than seen. The Reformation changed the focus of worship from the eye to the ear.

The Reformers saw the necessity and centrality of preaching. Each Sunday, when the Word of God was publicly read, Christ spoke. In the tradition of Ezra, who publicly read from the scroll in Nehemiah 8, and of Jesus, who entered a synagogue and took the scroll at the beginning of his ministry, the Protestants held that the Word of God was central to Christian formation. The Reformers were on to something: we must know the truth and remember the truth. This recognition of biblical centrality need not elevate the Bible to the point of reconstituting the Trinity, as in the oft-repeated quip "Father, Son, and Holy Scriptures." However, the Spirit of God is revealed in the Word of God. The Bible is the Spirit's means of grace for the people of God.

I came to faith in a tradition that valued and treasured the Bible. The pulpit was in the center of the worship space, and the sermon was the longest portion. The way of spiritual growth was through personal devotions and corporate Bible study. The rest of this book will be adding layers of formation to the foundation of truth. The Bible is important to spiritual formation because truth is important to spiritual formation. The way of blessedness is meditating on this law day and night—Psalm 1 is still true.

12. The role of the Reformation in the rise of literacy should not be missed. Martin Luther sought to offer public-school education to all German youth. The printing press was also important in the rise of literacy and the emphasis on schooling that resulted from the Reformation.

Each Sunday, we should come to church with an expectation that God is going to speak to the congregation. We should be on the edge of our seats as the preacher approaches the pulpit. Kids should see parents sitting with their Bibles open, attentive to what God is saying through his Word. Because when God speaks, things happen. The story of the dry bones in Ezekiel 37 is pivotal to my understanding of preaching. In many ways, the manner in which we move from death to life requires the prophetic word coming to us. The preaching of the Word of God is the means God uses to take dead people—really, super-dead people (very dry bones)—and breathe life into them. Spiritually, we are dead. But by the spoken Word, souls go from death to life and begin to walk and move about differently in the world. The message of grace makes us alive to the goodness of God. "Can these bones live?" God asks (Ezek. 37:3). The answer is yes—if God speaks.

HOLISTIC KNOWLEDGE AS WISDOM

While truth is the foundation, there are some inherent limitations to the truth tradition. In some streams, transformation can take a flattened form, as if knowing inevitably leads to doing. Sermons therefore become something like advice giving. "You should really believe this or do this." But we don't work in such a streamlined fashion. For example, do you know that sin is bad? Do you know you should pursue righteousness? Do you know you're forgiven? I'm guessing you have some degree of realization of these truths, yet that does not mean you have entirely stopped sinning. If only it were that easy!

Another limitation of the truth tradition is that the pursuit and propagation of truth are sometimes practiced according to a naturalistic approach that fails to factor in God's grace and that has no place for mystery and wonder: truth can be believed when it is certain, and it is certain when I explain it. This kind of tight rationalism is inadequate. Biblical truth does not explain away mystery but enhances it. We never "master" biblical truth; biblical truth masters us. The result is wonder and humility, not smugness and pride.

In this last section of the chapter, I want to expand our understanding of truth beyond mere knowledge to include wisdom. In seeking the truth, we are not trying to know more things as if we were studying for a test. Biblical literacy does not mean mere memorization. Knowing the Bible serves the purpose of helping us be rightly attached to the truths of Scripture.

Theologian Ellen Charry compares theology to medicine. There is such a thing as good practice of medicine and also such a thing as bad practice, or malpractice. The same is true in theology. First, good practice of medicine requires knowledge. Physicians undergo years of training in medical school, including exams, evaluations, and so on. Theology likewise requires knowledge, not only of the Scriptures but of church history, the creeds, and Christian tradition. We stand on the shoulders of our church fathers and mothers to see the Bible with greater clarity. Theologians need robust training and deep wells of resources from which to draw. Knowledge is foundational.

Second, good practice involves highly skilled judgment. Truth is not a static thing to be applied once for all; each situation calls for a different judgment. In medical practice, patients change and may not indicate the right symptoms if the doctor asks the wrong questions. And even if the doctor knows all the diseases in the world, they need to know how to discern and distinguish diseases. This requires skill that, in turn, requires practice. Likewise, in theology the truth of Scripture is unchanging, yet how that truth applies will be different based on whom the practitioner is applying the remedy to: Is this person doubting or prideful? Is she a new Christian or mature Christian? Is he young or old? We need skilled judgment to administer the gospel medicine rightly. We need to ask the right questions, provide honest answers, and see the situation clearly.

Third, Charry notes that good practice requires trust and obedience. Without a board certifying the doctor, the patient will not trust the diagnosis or remedy. We want to know that the person we are taking advice from is trustworthy, or we won't act on their information. Care, which is how one builds trust, is not an auxiliary component of theological practice but rather is essential. Everyone who is in the church long enough will meet an exceptionally smart Christian who knows a lot of the Bible but is a jerk. The truth they have is not the problem; the way they wield it is. Such people view gospel truth not as medicine but as a sword. We can usually tell that they love being right more than they love other people. It's hard to trust that kind of person. Good truth treatment must include care.[13]

In our journey to be wise theologians, the way we encounter the truth also impacts the wisdom we glean. The Bible is not a scientific textbook. You can read the text "literally" for certain reasons, yet you will be limited in the truths you find that way. A. W. Pink argues that there are many ways to read Scripture: educationally, professionally, historically, inquisitively, and so on. He maintains that though these ways of reading may add something to our understanding, they can be disordered ways of reading. Pink argues, "Our end in perusing His Word should be to learn how to please and glorify Him, and that, by our characters being formed under its holy influence and our conduct regulated in all its details by the rules He has there laid down. The mind needs instructing, but unless the conscience be searched, the heart influenced, the will moved, such knowledge will only puff us up and add to our condemnation."[14] Truth needs to take root not only in the head but also in the heart if it is to lead to true wisdom. If we know the truth but don't practice it, then we don't really know it.

CONCLUSION

As I mentioned earlier, I grew up in a tradition that loves the Bible—and rightfully so. I now belong to another tradition that also loves the Bible, but formation in this tradition, Anglicanism, is richer than "the Bible or bust." Nevertheless, Anglicanism has two foundational documents called the *Books of Homilies*. These books are compilations of sermons that parish priests read aloud to their churches to ensure consistent truth was proclaimed in their churches. The first sermon, called "A Fruitful Exhortation to the Reading of Holy

13. Before Paul tells Timothy about the Scriptures and tells him to preach the Word, he reminds Timothy that he has followed Paul and that Paul has endured great suffering (1 Tim. 3:10–4:3). The foundation of preaching is an exemplary life. The chief shepherd should also be the chief sufferer.

14. Pink, *Spiritual Growth*, 124. I'd recommend Pink's *Profiting from the Word of God* for more information on how to read Scripture in a way that feeds the soul as well as informs the mind.

Scripture," offers a reminder about how important truth is. The homily ends this way:

> Let us be glad to review this precious gift of our heavenly Father. Let us hear, read, and know these holy rules, injunctions, and statutes of our Christian religion, and upon that we have made profession to GOD at our baptism. Let us with fear and reverence lay up (in the chest of our hearts) these necessary and fruitful lessons. Let us night and day muse, and have meditation and contemplation in them. Let us ruminate, and (as it were) chew the cud, that we may have the sweet juice, spiritual effect, marrow, honey, kernel, taste, comfort and consolation of them (Ps. 56:4). Let us stay, quiet, and certify our consciences, with the most infallible certainty, truth, and perpetual assurance of them. Let us pray to GOD (the only author of these heavenly studies) that we may speak, think, believe, live and depart hence, according to the wholesome doctrine, and verities of them.
>
> And by that means, in this world we shall have GOD'S defense, favor, and grace, with the unspeakable solace of peace, and quietness of conscience, and after this miserable life, we shall enjoy the endless bliss and glory of heaven: which he grant us all that died for us all, Jesus Christ, to whom with the Father and the holy Ghost, be all honor and glory, both now and everlastingly.[15]

Yes and amen. It's the truth.

---

15. Lancashire, "Fruitful Exhortation to the Reading of Holy Scripture" (edited for clarity).

✳ 3 ✳

SAINT AUGUSTINE

FAITH SEEKING UNDERSTANDING

My sin was this, that I looked for pleasure, beauty, and truth not in him but in myself and in his other creatures, and the search led me instead to pain, confusion, and error.

—Saint Augustine, *Confessions*

My introduction to Saint Augustine came through his *Confessions*. Equal parts memoir, prayer, and theological reflection, *Confessions* defies easy categorization. Augustine reflects his life story in a prayer back to God and invites readers into his story. He opens the book with these famous words, which function as a sort of thesis statement: "You have made us for yourself, and our heart is restless until it rests in you."[1] The first long section of Augustine's story is one attempt after another of trying to quench this restlessness. For much of his life he attempts to find meaning, purpose, and rest outside of himself. Will academic accomplishments make him happy? Will fitting in satisfy him? Will sexual encounters provide the thing that causes his soul to rest? He goes on a search for satisfaction and comes up short with every attempt.

1. Augustine, *Confessions* 1.1.1 (Chadwick, 3).

It isn't until he comes to himself (to use words of the story of the prodigal son in Luke 15:17) that he comes to God. In all these external pursuits, God was within him, as God was the one who gave him life. Later in the *Confessions*, Augustine poetically writes, "Late have I loved you, beauty so old and so new: late have I loved you. And see, you were within and I was in the external world and sought you there. . . . You were with me, and I was not with you."[2] Elsewhere he suggests, "Do not go outward; return within yourself. In the inward man dwells truth."[3] As such, Augustine is known as one of the first philosophers of interiority.[4] Whereas philosophers previously discussed the outside world, Augustine discusses the world of his soul. He unearths his deep and hidden thought life. He reflects on his reflection. He provides a first-person standpoint in the pursuit of truth. This seems common today, but in his time Augustine changed the standpoint of truth-seeking in unique ways.

AUGUSTINE'S STORY

Augustine was born in 354 in Thagaste, which is in modern-day Algeria. He's a church father who emerges from North Africa. His father, Patrick, was a Roman, pagan town counselor and tax collector. Patrick desired to have his son pursue the career that Patrick had always dreamed of for himself. So, Augustine was sent to the best schools to study with the best teachers so he could be the smartest

2. Augustine, *Confessions* 10.27.38 (Chadwick, 201). Elsewhere in the *Confessions*, Augustine writes, "But you were more inward than my most inward part and higher than the highest element within me" (3.6.11; Chadwick, 43).

3. Augustine, *On Christian Belief* 39.72 (quoted in Taylor, *Sources of the Self*, 129).

4. In proto-Descartes fashion, Augustine wonders how he knows anything.
Reason: You who wish to know yourself, do you know that you exist?
Augustine: I do.
Reason: How so?
Augustine: I do not know.
Reason: Do you know that you think?
Augustine: I do.
Reason: Therefore that it is true that you think.
Augustine: Certainly.
Augustine, *Soliloquies* 2.1.1 (quoted in González, *Mestizo Augustine*, 53).

and most successful person. Let's call it an ancient plan for upward mobility meant to fulfill his parents' wishes.

His mother, Monica, was of African descent and was a devout Christian. Whereas Patrick may have been a demanding though distant father, Monica comes across at times as an overbearing mother. She wanted the best for her son and clung a bit tightly. Yet Augustine credits her prayer and nurture as the conduit and catalyst of his eventual faith. She was a wise and saintly woman.

In reflecting on his youth, Augustine describes an early episode in his life where he was with his friends near a pear orchard. Not yet ripe, the pears had no value. But Augustine and his friends schemed to steal them. He shamefully remembers, "My desire was to enjoy not what I sought by stealing but merely the excitement of thieving and the doing of what was wrong. . . . I had no motive for my wickedness except wickedness itself. It was foul, and I loved it."[5] Groupthink and peer pressure had powerful sway for young Augustine. As he reflects on this incident, he says he would never have done it by himself, but the power of friendship, the power of belonging and being approved, drove him to do the illicit action. He was a conundrum to himself, free yet bound in ways he could not understand.

Though he had some youthful distractions from school, he ended up being somewhat of a golden boy and star student. His hunger for recognition and approval—from father and friends—drove him to success. He was sent to Carthage to learn with the best, but here he had another hunger that emerged in his young adulthood: lust. In his own words, "All around me hissed a cauldron of illicit loves. As yet I had never been in love and I longed to love. . . . I was in love with love."[6] We can feel the teenage angst of lust in Augustine. He was in love with love. Perhaps we could say he was a hopeless romantic, but the romance he wanted was sexual experience. He wanted to be accepted, and if that meant feeling "love" in the arms of a woman after a one-night stand, that would do for the time being.

In spite of his distractions, Augustine excelled in his studies in Carthage because, as he describes it, he had a "delight in human

5. Augustine, *Confessions* 2.4.9 (Chadwick, 29).
6. Augustine, *Confessions* 3.1.1 (Chadwick, 35).

vanity."[7] He didn't necessarily care to be smart, but he sure wanted to be *seen* as smart. To use YouTube rhetoric, he wanted to "own them with logic" and "destroy his opponent." Whether his argument was true didn't matter as long as he won.

PRECONVERSIONS

Throughout Augustine's early life he underwent several "preconversions" that reoriented him to the world, and books were often the catalyst for these changes. The first book was Cicero's *Hortensius*. Augustine claimed that "the book changed my feelings. It altered my prayers, Lord, to be towards you yourself. It gave me different values and priorities. Suddenly every vain hope became empty to me, and I longed for the immortality of wisdom with an incredible ardour in my heart."[8] In all of his schooling, Augustine had thought the goal was to know more than others, or at least to win arguments against others. Who cared about philosophy (i.e., loving the truth)? Education had been a status symbol for Augustine. But Cicero changed Augustine's thoughts on education. Augustine didn't want merely to *seem* smart anymore; he wanted to *be* wise. In the end, truth would indeed lead to happiness—but not in the way Augustine planned.[9]

Another preconversion for Augustine came through reading the writings of Mani. Mani was the founder of a heretical sect called the Manicheans. In essence, Manicheanism was a philosophical system that taught a division of the world into two realms: good and evil. The body, as material, was evil, but the spirit was good. This belief system could account for the problem of evil. Good and evil were eternal, so they resided within humanity. Christians had a harder time explaining evil because they said God was eternal and good. Then how did evil come about? For Augustine, this strict logical system explained the universe. Explanation was the goal of the Manicheans: to explain away all mysteries, to know everything. Because Manicheans

7. Augustine, *Confessions* 3.4.7 (Chadwick, 38).
8. Augustine, *Confessions* 3.4.7 (Chadwick, 39).
9. As Étienne Gilson contends, "In [Augustine's] doctrine wisdom, the object of philosophy, is always identified with happiness" (Gilson, *Christian Philosophy of Saint Augustine*, 3).

believed in this strict, logical system, truth was available only to the superrational, a limited few. These interests—explaining things and being elite—fueled Augustine's desire to be right.

Manicheanism drove Augustine's self-confidence. He could master and improve himself by conquest. If he worked hard enough, studied long enough, exhibited enough self-control, he could control his destiny. He still had some lingering questions about Manicheanism, but he was told to wait until Faustus, a leading teacher of the day, came to town. Augustine did just that, but Faustus left him feeling underwhelmed. *This is the guy I've been waiting for?* He wondered. *He seems pretty average.* This interaction sent Augustine into an intellectual crisis. Maybe he had made a wrong choice.

Commenting on Augustine's predicament, David Brooks writes,

> Reason is not powerful enough to build intellectual systems or models to allow you to accurately understand the world around you or anticipate what is to come. Your willpower is not strong enough to successfully police your desires. . . . The problem, Augustine came to believe, is that if you think you can organize your own salvation you are magnifying the very sin that keeps you from it. To believe that you can be captain of your own life is to suffer the sin of pride.[10]

Augustine thought he could conquer his life, but he found his life conquered. In biblical language, rather than merely knowing God, he became known by God (Gal. 4:8–9).

CONVERSION

After his schooling in Carthage and brief teaching stints in Thagaste, Carthage, and Rome, Augustine's move to Milan sparked a brief interest in Christianity. He heard good things about the bishop there, a man named Ambrose. Augustine had always thought Scripture was a bit foolish, not as refined as the philosophical Cicero. He started going to church to hear Ambrose preach, not for the content but in the hopes of picking up some rhetorical tricks so he could be more convincing. But in spite of his intentions, Augustine realized that

10. Brooks, *Road to Character*, 199.

"while I opened my heart in noting the eloquence with which he [Ambrose] spoke, there also entered no less the truth which he affirmed, though only gradually."[11] Augustine's conversion was a slow burn.

In Ambrose, Augustine found someone he could trust. Truth depends on trust. The Quaker educator Parker Palmer explains the etymology of "truth." "The English word 'truth' comes from a Germanic root that also gives rise to our word 'troth,' as in the ancient vow 'I pledge thee my troth.' With this word one person enters a covenant with another, a pledge to engage in a mutually accountable and transforming relationship, a relationship forged of trust and faith in the face of unknowable risks."[12] Palmer points out that relationality connects to belief. We are not as intellectual and reasonable as we think we are. On Ambrose, philosopher James K. A. Smith notes, "From Ambrose, Augustine would realize that the Christianity he'd rejected was not Christianity. But it was Ambrose's love and welcome that created the intellectual space for him to even consider that."[13] Sometimes a good and faithful friend can give plausibility structures for belief—that is, the habits or ethos that makes something believable. Ambrose appears to have been not merely knowledgeable but also a wise theological physician.

One day, Augustine's life took a turn that changed him forever. By "coincidence" (as often is the case in transformative moments), he met a fellow African transplant in Milan named Pontianus. This man began telling Augustine about Christian saints, particularly Egyptian monks like Saint Anthony, who abandoned everything and lived in the desert to follow God. They weren't ashamed of the gospel. These stories convicted Augustine, as he was fearful of what commitment to Christ would mean for his social standing.

He rushed to his friend Alypius and wondered aloud about how the unlearned could teach masters of rhetoric anything. These simple people seemed to have conquered their passions while Augustine was "deeply disturbed in spirit, angry with indignation and distress."[14] Augustine seems to have been intellectually convinced of Christianity at this time. He didn't need more answers. Yet he had a greater

11. Augustine, *Confessions* 5.14.24 (Chadwick, 88).
12. Palmer, *To Know as We Are Known*, 31.
13. J. K. A. Smith, *On the Road with St. Augustine*, 152.
14. Augustine, *Confessions* 8.8.19 (Chadwick, 146).

problem. His affections for God lagged behind his mind. He didn't know whether he loved God even if he believed in him. Would belief be strong enough to conquer passions?

He then went outside Alypius's house to a garden. He describes his mental state as being like that of a madman with phantom limbs. He couldn't control himself. It looked as if Augustine was on the verge of a mental breakdown.

Yet it wasn't mental. What was holding him back was not an existential crisis but sin. Those old lusts came and spoke. "Vain trifles and the triviality of the empty-headed, my old loves, held me back. They tugged at the garment of my flesh and whispered, 'Are you getting rid of us? . . . From this moment we shall never be with you again, not for ever and ever.' . . . Meanwhile the overwhelming force of habit was saying to me: 'Do you think you can live without them?'"[15] Isn't that how sin talks? "You think you can give me up? Forever? Never again?"

Underneath a fig tree,[16] he pondered, "'How long, how long is it going to be?' 'Tomorrow, tomorrow.' 'Why not now? Why not an end to my impure life in this very hour?'" Augustine was confronted with a decision. He then began to hear what sounded like a chant or kids' song: *Tolle lege, tolle lege*, or "Pick up and read, pick up and read." Books are a prevalent part of Augustine's story.

Supposing this chant to be a divine call to open the book in Alypius's house (which "happened" to be the Epistle to the Romans), he rushed back. He picked up the book, flipped it open, and read wherever his eyes "happened" to land: "Let us walk properly as in the daytime, not in orgies and drunkenness, not in sexual immorality and sensuality, not in quarreling and jealousy. But put on the Lord Jesus Christ, and make no provision for the flesh, to gratify its desires" (Rom. 13:13–14). Augustine writes, "I neither wished nor needed to read further. At once, with the last words of this sentence, it was as if a light of relief from all anxiety flooded into my heart. All the shadows of doubt were dispelled."[17] The truth of the Bible gave Augustine the rest he had been longing for.

15. Augustine, *Confession*, 8.11.26 (Chadwick, 151).
16. The garden imagery in this story and his earlier account of taking from the pear tree should not be lost on us.
17. Augustine, *Confessions* 8.12.29 (Chadwick, 153).

Augustine had thought he was the master of his own destiny and shaper of his own thought. He had thought his intellectual system could bring him to God. But he kept finding himself unreliable. So, he made the leap toward truth. "Why are you relying on yourself, only to find yourself unreliable? Cast yourself upon him, do not be afraid. He will not withdraw himself so that you fall. Make the leap without anxiety; he will catch you and heal you."[18] The truth set Augustine free. The truth caught and healed him.

His conversion led to a posture of receptiveness. When God offers us a gift, we try to buy it. All of Augustine's life, he had wanted to earn his prestige. Yet he found that prestige was a gift and not a wage. The reality of grace is central to the Christian mindset, and as you may remember from chapter 2, all great religious revivals start with the centrality of grace. Grace seems too simple, too accessible for someone as talented and smart as Augustine. Grace would mean Augustine wasn't special or more capable than others in regard to salvation. For most of his early life, he couldn't accept that. However, Augustine came to the end of himself, and there he found God.

TRUTH AS A TOOL, NOT A WEAPON

Augustine's conversion set him on a path of Christian contemplation, careful study, and religious dialogue. He wanted to be left alone for a life of leisurely learning, but once the gospel took root, it moved outward. As Justo González writes, "It was not only now a matter of studying for the love of truth, or as an act of devotion, but also of studying as preparation to teach others."[19] Augustine saw the needs around him and was compelled (and somewhat forced) into the priesthood and, eventually, to being a bishop.

After the garden scene, Augustine got to writing and didn't stop. Today, Augustine's collected writings take up forty-four volumes. He wrote more than many of us will ever read, and he did it in a day without computers, typewriters, or a printing press. It's astonishing to think about. The impressiveness does not come merely from the

18. Augustine, *Confessions* 8.11.27 (Chadwick, 151).
19. González, *Mestizo Augustine*, 75.

amount he wrote, either. Those within and outside the Christian faith consider him one of the greatest philosophical minds. While his writing is quantitatively impressive, it is because of the *quality* of his work that he is still shaping conversation today.

Like many church fathers, Augustine was an apologist: he defended the faith from false doctrine, guarding the deposit entrusted to him (see 1 Tim. 6:20). He gave himself away to the truth that found him. His first writings refuted his former sect, the Manicheans, rebutting key tenets and arguing with key leaders. He then moved from the Manicheans to the Donatists, who had emerged after persecution in the early church. The church had to figure out what to do with those who had reneged on their faith during a time of persecution and then wanted to come back to the church once the persecution was over. Having denied Christ, would they be allowed back when it was easier to be a Christian? The Donatists were against that. Those who avoided persecution or martyrdom should not be considered Christians. Donatists were seeking a pure church, one uncorrupted by sin and error.

Augustine's tone changed significantly when he addressed the Donatists. Earlier in his life he had wanted to win arguments, but here he dealt respectfully with this group, "for his purpose was not to defeat his readers but to convince them."[20] Augustine realized that people argue from their heart more than their mind. "Their love for truth takes the form that they love something else and want this object of their love to be the truth; and because they do not wish to be deceived, they do not wish to be persuaded that they are mistaken," writes Augustine. "And so they hate the truth for the sake of the object they love instead of the truth. They love the truth for the light it sheds, but hate it when it shows them up as being wrong."[21] He came to these insights because he had studied his own heart. He had also wanted to be seen as being "in the know." There's a certain type of academic I call the "Well, Actuallys," who are always out to correct people because they know everything. When someone says, "We got there around 3:00," the "Well, Actually" chimes in, "Well,

20. González, *Mestizo Augustine*, 111.
21. Augustine, *Confessions* 10.23.24 (Chadwick, 199–200).

actually, it was more like 3:15." I don't know Augustine's personality, but I imagine him being one of those people in his preconversion days.

But in his postconversion days Augustine tried to convince by caring. He was concerned less with being right and more with caring for people with the truth. He ceased to weaponize truth. Philippe de Champaigne painted a fitting portrait of Augustine in 1650. *Veritas* (truth) is symbolized by a sun in the top-left corner. The rays of truth proceed from the sun, through Augustine's head, to his heart, which he holds in his hand on the right side of the painting. This image is an apt illustration of Augustine's thought. Truth doesn't end in the head but makes its way to the control center, which is the heart. He understood the heart as being central to our living. What someone loves is more important than what they can consciously know or express. Truth is foundational but insufficient. As David Brooks writes, "Knowledge is not enough for tranquillity and goodness, because it doesn't contain the motivation to be good. Only love impels action. We don't become better because we acquire new information. We become better because we acquire better loves. We don't become what we know. Education is a process of love formation."[22] Augustine was conquered by love, and he sought to convince others with love and truth. Knowledge needed to turn to wisdom.

The last major doctrinal controversy Augustine faced started with Pelagius, perhaps Augustine's most well-known debate partner. Pelagians said that accountability required choice. God couldn't hold people accountable if they were sinful by nature. If sin wasn't a choice but was how humans were born, then God would be unjust to hold them accountable. For this reason Pelagians denied original sin, the doctrine that people are born in a state of sin. But Augustine knew the depth of sin in his heart. Pelagius was attacking the gospel itself as well as the glory of God in salvation. Augustine understood that we humans are unable to choose Christ in our sinful state. The will is bound to sin, and without God's intervention, sin is all we choose. Humans need God to act to save us. He's the one who gives the gift. All we can do is receive.

22. Brooks, *Road to Character*, 211.

Augustine was asked why so much of his writing dealt with Pelagianism. Here's how he responded: "First and foremost because no subject gives me greater pleasure. For what ought to be more attractive to us sick men, than grace, grace by which we are healed; for us lazy men, than grace, grace by which we are stirred up; for us men longing to act, than grace, by which we are helped?"[23] In the Roman Catholic Church, Augustine has come to be known as the doctor of grace. I can't think of a better theme to mark a life.

At the end of his life, he went back through his work and made some retractions. He was humble enough to detail how his mind had changed throughout the years, what he had overstated or underemphasized, and what he had been just plain wrong about. For Augustine, truth was not something that he held; truth held him. Truth affected him deeply, and it caused a loving overflow to others. He dedicated his life to the truth that gave his soul rest.[24]

---

23. Augustine, *Epistle 186*, 12.39 (quoted in Brown, *Augustine of Hippo*, 356).

24. For a fuller account of Augustine's philosophical foundations, see Gilson, *Christian Philosophy of Saint Augustine*.

PRACTICES

BIBLE STUDY

Perhaps the most popular form of spiritual formation in the evangelical world, Bible study allows us to know, interpret, and apply Scripture. When studying the Bible, we don't merely study; we allow the Word to study us. As we saw in chapter 1, the foundation of all spiritual formation is biblical truth. We ought to be devoted to studying the Bible.

SCRIPTURE MEMORIZATION

The Psalms instruct us to meditate on the law day and night. How is that possible if we don't know it? Memorizing Scripture is a way to meditate on the text when we don't have the Bible in hand. Jesus quotes the Bible when tempted by the devil, so memorizing the Bible is also a help in fighting sin.

LISTENING TO SERMONS

"Faith comes from hearing" (Rom. 10:17). The Word addresses us, but we need help in understanding it. Listening to the Bible being explained has been a formative habit for me, and it is a means of grace by which God changes us.

SINGING SCRIPTURAL SONGS

One further way to meditate on Scripture or biblical themes is to sing songs. One of the most beautiful things I've seen is older Christians with dementia still recalling the songs of their youth even when they have forgotten much else. Music is a great means of remembrance.

RESOURCES

Augustine. *On Christian Teaching*. Translated by R. P. H. Green. New York: Oxford University Press, 2008.

Charry, Ellen. *By the Renewing of Your Minds: The Pastoral Function of Christian Doctrine*. New York: Oxford University Press, 1997.

Lovelace, Richard. *Renewal as a Way of Life: A Guidebook for Spiritual Growth*. Eugene, OR: Wipf & Stock, 2002.

Robinson, Marilynne. *Gilead*. New York: Picador, 2006.

PART 2

GOODNESS

THE VIRTUOUS LIFE

I take it to be crucial that Christians must live in a manner that their lives are unintelligible if the God we worship in Jesus Christ does not exist.

—Stanley Hauerwas

So that he [Jesus] might present the church to himself in splendor, without spot or wrinkle or any such thing, that she might be holy and without blemish.

—Ephesians 5:27

✳ 4 ✳

In PURSUIT of the GOOD LIFE

RIGHTEOUSNESS WITHOUT SELF-RIGHTEOUSNESS

For most of my life I thought theology was the way to maturity. So, I read, and I studied, and then I read some more. The call to ministry was a call to prepare, and I was preparing my mind for sharp theological precision and deep sermons.

The first real ministry job I had was in Austin, Texas. Don and Jane were a couple in their eighties at the church. In 1970, they arrived in Guatemala as missionaries to the indigenous K'iche' population. There were less than twenty Christians when they arrived. When Don and Jane left in retirement twenty-seven years later, there were 32,000 Christians and 250 churches. I arrived in Austin with the ability to parse Greek verbs. Somehow that didn't feel the same. I may have had more theological training than Don and Jane, but their staggering numbers aside, they were holier than I was. Their joy was abundant. Their work was fruitful. My joy was minuscule. My work was just starting.

Jim became one of my best friends at that same church in Austin. He was in his late forties, whereas I was in my midtwenties. We were not alike. Jim had a rough childhood that he escaped by joining the military. He was training with the Army Rangers before he was dishonorably discharged for hitting his superior. He went on to join a biker gang and was a mule for drug smugglers. He ended up in jail for bank robbery. When he first came to church at the beckoning of his wife, he went up to the pastor and said something along the lines of, "This church thing is fine for my wife, but I won't believe a damn word of it." Jesus has a good sense of humor, I guess. It did not matter whether Jim believed in Jesus. Jesus came for Jim. He had grown up in a harder life than I had. He had been a Christian for less time than I had. I had read way more books than he had. Yet it seemed that Jim was more generous, more servant-hearted, and more loving than I was. He seemed to desire Jesus more than I did.

I also have a friend from high school named Logan. Logan lives in low-income housing in Charlotte, North Carolina, with his wife, Jessie. Most of the complex is filled with recent refugees from various countries. Jessie and Logan don't merely show up to serve these people; they live among them. They help feed children. Logan helps the adults fill out paperwork that they can't read. He meaningfully employs many of the kids he's worked with over the years. Jessie homeschools a few teenagers whom the public school system has left behind. I have two advanced degrees, and Logan likely hasn't thought about education since his last college class. Though I have more theological education, Logan and Jessie have more patience and kindness than anyone I've ever met. Logan puts people at ease with his presence. I love God with my mind, but Logan and Jessie seemed to be loving their neighbors with their whole being. I could give you all the theological reasons to care for the poor and vulnerable, yet Logan and Jessie actually care for the poor and vulnerable.

Considering these friends, at some point I had to ask myself: *What was I missing?* I had crossed my theological *t*'s and dotted my justification *j*'s. I had my degrees and a library full of books that I had (mostly) read. I had great, lofty ideas of God, yet my character was still lowly. I had not advanced as much as I knew I should have. My brain and my body seemed at odds.

In the truth tradition, people must believe to be saved. All else flows from believing the truth. Knowing leads to action. Meaning leads to practice. Yet these friends of mine led lives of extraordinary service and love without knowing as much as I did. Was my pursuit of truth the problem? Was I doing it wrong? Was it me? What was I supposed to do after I believed the truth?

The theologian N. T. Wright has written a book to answer that last question. It's aptly called *After You Believe*, and that title addresses a good question: What's the point of life after we believe in the truth of the gospel? Sometimes, in the truth tradition, truth can function like fire insurance. "I've believed already. What more do you want from me, God?" But following Christ is not about doing the bare minimum to get by; rather, it's about doing that which brings maximum health to one's soul. The goal for the Christian life is not merely about getting to heaven through believing true things. Salvation is a broader concept. The central question is this: What does it mean to live a life aimed toward God? This question is answered not by assent to some intellectual propositions but by ways of being and by habits.

Wright argues that the goal of life "after you believe" is to grow in character, or virtue. Having character is distinct from following a set of external rules or authentically living out some internal values. Rather, character "will generate the sort of behavior that rules might have pointed toward but which a 'rule-keeping' *mentality* can never achieve. And it will produce the sort of life which will in fact be true to itself—though the 'self' to which it will at last be true is the redeemed self, the transformed self, not the merely 'discovered' self of popular thought."[1] Character, or virtue, is about shaping instinctual reactions. The goal is to be a certain type of person who chooses to be gracious or merciful without straining or thinking about it. Those characteristics will be simply part of who the person is. Living a good life means living a life of character, living into one's redeemed self.

In the classical conception, there are three steps to developing virtue or character: glimpse the goal, work out the path toward it, and develop the habits needed to practice it.[2] This chapter focuses on

1. Wright, *After You Believe*, 7.
2. Wright, *After You Believe*, 170.

the first step: What is the goal of the Christian life? The next chapter addresses the path toward it. At the end of this book, it'll be up to you to practice the habits needed.

First Corinthians 13 is known as the chapter of love. Many have heard this chapter read at a wedding. I suppose it can apply to marital love, but that's not Saint Paul's immediate context. In 1 Corinthians 12 and 14, Paul discusses spiritual gifts. And in chapter 13 he puts forward the best and highest spiritual gift. More to be desired than prophecy or speaking in tongues or service or healing is the divine gift that we should all seek out: love. A life of love is the way of the Christian. A believer can be smart, kind, hardworking, and theologically astute, but if they don't have love, they're useless.

Here's how Saint Augustine defines the virtuous life:

> But living a just and holy life requires one to be capable of an objective and impartial evaluation of things: to love things, that is to say, in the right order, so that you do not love what is not to be loved, or fail to love what is to be loved, or have a greater love for what should be loved less, or an equal love for things that should be loved less or more, or a lesser or greater love for things that should be loved equally.[3]

Key to Augustine's conception of a good life ("a just and holy life") is the idea of ordered love. People can love a good thing in a wrong way, and that love can end up being destructive. If I love my wife more than I love God, then I'll put expectations on her that will always lead to disappointment, and I'll never be happy. And she'll be exhausted from trying to carry a burden that no person can bear.

Or if I love my job more than I love my kids, then I may have great success in teaching students, but my own children will be distant from me. I may be happy at work but miserable at home. There's nothing wrong with loving my wife or loving my job, but if it's in the wrong order, then my life will be disordered. That's not a good life! It's only when I have the foundation of loving God and loving my neighbor that my other loves can follow in a healthy order. It's our only hope of a good life. Ordered love is the rest that Saint Augustine has in mind.

3. Augustine, *On Christian Teaching*, 21.

THE STORY OF GOODNESS IN THE BIBLE

In the beginning, God creates goodness in everything. Stars, good. Water, good. Trees, good. Sharks? Also good. Heck, maybe even mosquitoes (though I have my doubts). God invites people to enjoy his good creation in a cosmic act of hospitality: take and eat.

But the serpent causes Adam and Eve to doubt the goodness of God. Maybe obedience to God is a limitation rather than freedom. Maybe he's keeping something good from them. So rather than obey the Creator, Adam and Eve trust a creature instead. Hebrew scholar Dru Johnson suggests, "In order to know, you must listen to trusted authorities and do what they say in order to see what they are showing you."[4] Rather than do what God told them in order to see what he was showing them, our first parents did what the serpent told them, and as a result, they saw their shame. We fall prey to the same trap. We listen to the deceptive voice of the serpent, and we see our shame. We all exchange the love of God for the love of creatures, with the same result.

But God does not reject Adam and Eve; rather, he makes them a promise. An offspring will rise to crush the head of that wicked serpent. God continues to be gracious and patient. The reason he chooses the descendants of Abraham and Isaac and Jacob is not their might or wisdom. They are the losers of the bunch! God chooses this group of people because he loves them and is keeping his promise (Deut. 7:7–8).

God's gracious choice of Israel leads to a choice being given to the people of Israel. After leading the people out of Egypt into the promised land, a new type of garden, God lays out the stipulations. He saves, and this is what it means to be God's saved people: to be like God and to represent him to the watching world. God calls Israel to be holy as he is holy (Lev. 11:45). Before they enter the promised land, the people of Israel gather on Mount Ebal in Moab. On the mountaintop they receive a promise from God. If they obey, things will go well. If they disobey, they will be cursed. Who will they listen to: the pagan gods currently worshiped in that land or the God of creation? In summary, Moses writes this:

> For this commandment that I command you today is not too hard for you, neither is it far off. It is not in heaven, that you should say, "Who

4. Johnson, *Scripture's Knowing*, 16.

will ascend to heaven for us and bring it to us, that we may hear it and do it?" Neither is it beyond the sea, that you should say, "Who will go over the sea for us and bring it to us, that we may hear it and do it?" But the word is very near you. It is in your mouth and in your heart, so that you can do it.

See, I have set before you today life and good, death and evil. If you obey the commandments of the LORD your God that I command you today, by loving the LORD your God, by walking in his ways, and by keeping his commandments and his statutes and his rules, then you shall live and multiply, and the LORD your God will bless you in the land that you are entering to take possession of it. But if your heart turns away, and you will not hear, but are drawn away to worship other gods and serve them, I declare to you today, that you shall surely perish. You shall not live long in the land that you are going over the Jordan to enter and possess. I call heaven and earth to witness against you today, that I have set before you life and death, blessing and curse. Therefore choose life, that you and your offspring may live, loving the LORD your God, obeying his voice and holding fast to him, for he is your life and length of days, that you may dwell in the land that the LORD swore to your fathers, to Abraham, to Isaac, and to Jacob, to give them. (Deut. 30:11–20)

According to Moses, obeying God is possible. It's not too hard or far off. Do you want good things? Then obey. Do you want to avoid curses? Then follow God. It's a simple decision. Would you rather live, or die? If we're in our right mind, it's not complicated. I'll take life, please!

But the story of Israel is a story of failure. They choose to worship foreign gods and neglect the strangers in their midst. They do not take care of the land but instead exploit it. They fail to be a holy nation. Their disobedience results in a failure to love God and neighbor and a neglect of their gifted land. Every aspect of existence that was good is now broken. The people of Israel choose death.

Like Israel, we know the right thing to do. It's not too hard for us. Yet we choose death over and over and over. Why do we make choices that kill us, that lead us further from God and increase our isolation from others, and that bring us the crippling shame that accompanies sin? It doesn't make sense.

Jesus enters our confusion and shows us a good life, a flourishing life. When Pontius Pilate presents Jesus to the crowd before his crucifixion, he uses the phrase "Behold the man!" (John 19:5). Like numerous other people in the Bible, Pilate has said more than he intended. He is delivering Jesus to his death, but he is also pointing to the quintessential man, the man we should all see and desire to become. Jesus is the model to which we are to conform. He is wise, and his wisdom leads to obedience. He bears the curses of Deuteronomy on our behalf. Jesus comes to suffer the consequences of our sin, and he gives us the blessing he deserved. Jesus consistently obeys the law that we broke, so that we can receive his obedience.

Jesus invites his followers to a full life. He doesn't want us to meet the bare-minimum requirements for heavenly entry. He wants us to walk in such a way that we will sense the kingdom of God. He desires that his followers live full, flourishing, happy lives, even now. Christianity is not merely a truth claim. It's a way of life. The truth claims of the gospel have horizontal dimensions. If God loves us, then we are to love one another (1 John 4:7–11, 19). As W. H. Auden poetically puts it, "You shall love your crooked neighbour / With your crooked heart."[5] Our love does not depend on whether we or others have our lives in order.

RESTORING THE "GOOD" IN THE GOOD LIFE

In the Gospel of Luke a lawyer comes up to Jesus, wrestling with an issue that's similar to the one Deuteronomy presents: choosing a way that leads to life rather than death. He wants to know what he must do to inherit eternal life. In Christian culture this phrase "eternal life" is often quickly filtered to mean life after death. It is a quantity of time that is forever. And that's true enough. But it also has connotations of the quality of life. Eternal life is a *kind* of life worth living. This young lawyer wants to know how to live forever, sure, but he also wants a flourishing life—full, lasting life, life that leads not toward death and destruction but toward life everlasting.

Jesus, being the good teacher that he is, flips the question around. He asks what the young lawyer thinks. And the lawyer gives the right theological answer: "You shall love the Lord your God with all your

5. Auden, "As I Walked Out One Evening," 135.

heart and with all your soul and with all your strength and with all your mind, and your neighbor as yourself" (Luke 10:27).

Bingo. Jesus says that the young lawyer is right. If you want a full life, if you want lasting joy beyond temporal happiness, if you want to make choices that lead to goodness and beauty, love God and neighbor. Order your loves. Choose life. It's not too hard. It's not too far off. The word is near. It's simple. Go and love.

But the lawyer has a clarifying question: "And who is my neighbor?" What a brilliant question! If I can define "neighbor" however I want, the task becomes easier. I can be kind to people who vote like me. I can show mercy to those in my economic class. I can offer hospitality to those who can repay the favor. I can love those who share my interests. I can be nice to those who are nice to me.

In response, Jesus tells a story that makes "neighbor" a concrete reality instead of an abstract concept (Luke 10:30–37). Who is my neighbor in practice? In the story a man traveling from Jerusalem to Jericho is beaten up on the side of the road and left for dead.

Two religious figures, a priest and a Levite, pass by and don't offer help. But then comes a Samaritan—one of those outcast half-breeds whom the Israelites hate. He goes to the man who was beat up, binds his wounds, pours oil and wine on him, puts him on a donkey, and takes him to an inn. The Samaritan tells the innkeeper that he will come back and cover the cost of whatever they spend.

Martin Luther King Jr. famously preached on this passage. He told of the mountainous and dangerous terrain of this road to Jericho, where thieves and robbers often hid out in search of an unsuspecting traveler. In closing, he offered these words:

> And you know, it's possible that the priest and the Levite looked over that man on the ground and wondered if the robbers were still around. Or it's possible that they felt that the man on the ground was merely faking. And he was acting like he had been robbed and hurt, in order to seize them over there, lure them there for quick and easy seizure. And so the first question that the priest asked—the first question that the Levite asked was, "If I stop to help this man, what will happen to me?" But then the Good Samaritan came by. And he reversed the question: "If I do not stop to help this man, what will happen to him?"[6]

6. King, "Three Dimensions of a Complete Life."

This latter question animates this text: If I don't stop, what will happen to this person in front of me? If I don't offer kindness? If I don't use my voice and power to speak up and do something? If I don't love them? How do I bring life to those around me?

Jesus ends the parable with a final question: "Which of these three, do you think, proved to be a neighbor to the man who fell among the robbers?" (Luke 10:36). The lawyer can't even muster the words to say "the Samaritan," his hatred of neighbor is so strong. All he can respond is, "The one who showed him mercy" (Luke 10:37).

So, back to the question of choosing life: Which way is eternal life? Jesus flips the idea of a flourishing life upside down. The first question regarding a life well lived is not what makes someone happy or what's in it for them. Rather, the first question is how you may bring happiness to those around you. Virtue is about turning to others in love. Here is eternal life: loving God in such a way that it pours out into love of the vulnerable and needy, caring for the poor and suffering, offering gracious hospitality to those who may never repay. This is eternal life.

Elsewhere, Jesus says that loving God is like loving oneself.[7] Indeed, once we see our neighbor as made in the image of God, the connection to loving God becomes clear and convicting. How we treat our neighbors is an indication of what we think of God. Or as Dorothy Day urges, "I really only love God as much as I love the person I love the least."[8] Ouch. To turn away from loving our neighbor is to turn away from God.

The challenge in the good life is pursuing righteousness without self-righteousness. The good (and difficult) news is that grace ruins self-righteousness. Grace levels the playing field. Grace means that we are all equally flawed and eternally distant from the Father. Grace generates true humility, which does not seek praise or credit from others but ascribes righteousness where it is due. Paul asks a great

7. "Teacher, which is the great commandment in the Law?" And he said to him, "You shall love the Lord your God with all your heart and with all your soul and with all your mind. This is the great and first commandment. *And a second is like it*: You shall love your neighbor as yourself. On these two commandments depend all the Law and the Prophets" (Matt. 22:36–40).

8. Day repeated this line on several occasions in her "On Pilgrimage" column in the *Catholic Worker* magazine.

rhetorical question in 1 Corinthians 4:7: "What do you have that you did not receive?" The answer, of course, is "Nothing." We receive everything we have and are. Our grace-driven effort does not earn God's favor. It doesn't make us better than others. It's not about comparison at all. This side of heaven, we will never attain perfection, but we "press on to make it [our] own, because Christ Jesus has made [us] his own" (Phil. 3:12). Or as Paul says earlier in Philippians, "Work out your own salvation with fear and trembling, for it is God who works in you, both to will and to work for his good pleasure" (2:12–13). We work, knowing that God is already at work. God is the one who does all things, so he gets the credit and glory for whatever progress we make.

As we pursue righteousness, there will always be a struggle to be *authentically* good rather than *superficially* good, to be and not to seem. I grew up playing soccer. Sometimes you can look at a person and tell whether they are good. They carry a confidence and have a swagger that tells others they are who they seem to be. Other times, looks can be deceiving. There are some people who look like Cristiano Ronaldo but are outed as posers when the ball comes near them. They may have the look and the gear, but they lack the substance. They've spent money to curate an image but avoided the hard work that develops excellence. The same can be true of our spiritual lives. The pursuit of goodness is about being truly good rather than pretending or playing a part.

THE GOODNESS OF THE LORD'S SUPPER

When we take the Lord's Supper, God invites us into the good life of communion. We take goodness within our mouths, chew it, and digest it, and it becomes part of us. In our understanding of goodness we see that knowledge is more than intellectual. There's a habitual or ritual shape to knowledge. To draw again on N. T. Wright, the way virtue is formed is through habitual action. The Lord's Supper comes to feed us habitually. The ritual of remembrance shapes us to be a certain kind of people; we remember a sacrificial love so that we might become sacrificial people. As Christ is broken and given, so we break and give of ourselves for others. We are changed through this action as well as by our remembering. The Lord's Supper forms us in virtue by our ritual participation.

In many ways the Lord's Supper is a reversal of the fall. Our first parents followed the wisdom of the serpent and saw its consequence. When the serpent said to take and eat the fruit of the tree in the midst of the garden, they took and ate. And they saw their shame. Jesus offers another option. He offers us his very flesh and his very blood. The wisdom of Christ is the way that leads to life. Do this, and you will live. Take and eat.

CONCLUSION

I began this chapter with a few examples of my friends who were less theologically learned yet more virtuous than I was. They exemplified kindness and joy and patience while I felt that I was floundering, trying to find some footholds for my beliefs. I lived from my head and needed to enact my embodiment. My beliefs and my commitments needed to take shape, to be incarnated. As much as Christianity is a belief system, it is also a way of life. After all, Christ saves not by his words but by his life and his actions. I needed help putting my beliefs and words into practice.

The good news is that Christianity has a rich history of practices and habits that form Christians. They don't earn our salvation, but they do provide a way of life that we don't have to make up. The goal of growing in virtue is for us to become the type of people who are Christlike even without having to think about it. Responding with grace and love can become second nature when the story of Christianity is so much a part of us. The aim is that we develop Christlike character. My friends taught me by their lives more than by their lips. My friends gave me a vision of a life well lived. In growing up into Christ, I needed to see in order to know.

Having a worthy goal is the first step of character formation. Now we need to know which habits get us there.

✳ 5 ✳

HOW DO WE BECOME VIRTUOUS?

THE POWER OF HABIT

We are saved by grace of course, and by it alone, and not because we deserve it. That is the basis of God's acceptance of us. But grace does *not* mean that sufficient strength and insight will be automatically 'infused' into our being in the moment of need. . . . A baseball player who expects to excel in the game without adequate exercise of his body is no more ridiculous than the Christian when put to the test without the appropriate exercise in godly living.

—Dallas Willard, *The Spirit of the Disciplines*

Not long ago I saw an advertisement on social media. A new Bible-study plan hit the market. Featuring a young man who had once grown stale in his Bible reading, this ad claimed the Bible study transformed his life as soon as he started it. It *completely* changed his spiritual life.

Maybe it did. But I tend to be skeptical of quick-fix spirituality. If a new consumer good creates immediate transformation, I question the depth of that transformation. A deep spirituality is less like a love-at-first-sight infatuation and more like the hard-won love of an enduring marriage. Growing with God is a marriage, not a fling. As Jennifer Herdt notes in her book on virtue, "It is not through an instantaneous evangelical rebirth, a lightning bolt from heaven, that Christians are made [virtuous], but through hearing the scriptures that proclaim the story of God with us and participating in the practices of the church constituted by its willingness to be defined by that story."[1] As Christians, we grow through participation in the regular means of grace. Sometimes we sense our growth, and it's exciting, like lightning. Other times, the same growth can seem like a carrot growing—underground, unseen, unnoticed, undetected.

In my youth I was sold the "mountaintop experience" form of spirituality. The next big thing defined the life of faith. A retreat would help me grow. A conference would be the catalyst of maturity. Doing something new and exciting was the way to sustain faith. I'm all for those things, but as I've gotten older, I've realized the value of daily, habitual, unsexy rituals. Spiritual writer Tish Harrison Warren says, "The crucible of our formation is in the monotony of our daily routines."[2] Indeed, as Ronald Rolheiser writes, "Love and prayer can only be sustained through ritual, routine, and rhythm."[3] I've learned that showing up is half the battle.

The energy and enthusiasm of the moment you first believed are impossible to sustain. Seeking such a spirituality would be like, after sixty years of marriage, expecting to have the same butterflies one had in a budding romance. But that's not how love works. As I write these words, I've been married only eight years, and I don't have those butterflies anymore. But I love my wife a lot more now than I did eight years ago.

When things get stale, dry, and boring, what will sustain a life of faith (or love)? No one can be interesting, lively, or emotionally compelling all the time. Life is filled with the mundane and normal. Rolheiser writes, "What sustains a relationship long-term is ritual,

1. Herdt, *Putting on Virtue*, 350.
2. Warren, *Liturgy of the Ordinary*, 24.
3. Rolheiser, *Domestic Monastery*, 41.

routine, a regular rhythm that incarnates the commitment."[4] Habits incarnate commitment.

THE PROBLEM OF GOODNESS AFTER THE REFORMATION

I know how unexciting and deadening and inauthentic the word "ritual" sounds. Early in ministry I was meeting with a younger man who had fallen on some hard times. His faith, which had once been strong, now seemed weak. Struggles with sin that he thought were long gone had come back with a force he'd never experienced. I wanted to schedule a regular meeting with him. But to him the idea of scheduling a meeting sounded so . . . ritualistic. If I really loved and valued him, he thought, I would just text him because I wanted to hang out. Putting a meeting on the calendar robbed our relationship of spontaneity and therefore of the affection that drives relationship.

I understand that sentiment to some extent. When I was younger I had enough margin that I could text someone on a free Tuesday afternoon to see what they were up to. Yet as I've gotten older and time has become more squeezed, I have realized the importance of ritual and habits. Scheduling a meeting does not stifle love but rather stimulates it so that it flourishes. If I don't schedule it, I'll be too distracted or busy to think about it. I may not *want* to do it in the moment, and I may not *think* to do it if it's not scheduled. But if I truly value something in my life, then the way that incarnates itself is in a habit or practice.

The issue of authenticity and virtue presents itself in the Reformation as well. Doesn't this talk of virtue seem like works righteousness? Isn't this ritualistic religion what Martin Luther railed against after he had wrestled with guilt and shame and the question of how he could be accepted by God? Don't these rituals negate grace?

There is indeed a danger in pursuing goodness when we think we can make ourselves good or that goodness consists of our own effort. The temptation to work for affection, to do something special

---

4. Rolheiser, *Domestic Monastery*, 44.

so that God will love us, to prove ourselves worthy of God's love is ever present. It's a real thing.

The reason we desire goodness matters. The premises and meaning of actions are important because truth matters (see part 1). Is the habit meant to earn God's love? If so, that practice is anti-gospel and anti-grace. Is it out of obligation? If so, isn't it inauthentic? Shouldn't we act by what we feel? And who can tell me what to do anyway?

Today I find a version (or perversion) of Christianity that stands at the opposite extreme from Luther and the Reformation. As I talk to young people, the most common misperception I encounter is that God doesn't really care about what we do because he knows what's in our hearts. They seem to think that Christianity is a belief system rather than a way of life, as if God cares that we believe in the gospel but is indifferent to what we regularly do. He's not concerned about those outside things or external actions—that's religion. All he cares about are interior intentions and relationship. Believing is the bare minimum of flourishing, and that's all God would ask of us. Leave my life alone.

After all (so this line of thought goes), Luther thought that no external practice or imitation of an exemplar could produce the righteousness of God. Such actions are seen as fake, superficial. "Rather," as Jennifer Herdt describes this thinking, "the starting point must be a moment of utter passivity, in which we relinquish any reliance on human agency. We must not begin 'acting the part' of virtue but instead *seeming* to be what we *are* in fact—sinful."[5] To pretend to be virtuous would be to put confidence in one's ability rather than in the righteousness of God. Isn't practicing virtue inauthentic if we don't feel it? Going to church when we don't want to would make us hypocrites, right?

Both ideas—that habits negate grace and that God cares only about interior intentions—are understandable but misguided. Truth and goodness are intimately connected. In part 1 of the book, we looked at how beliefs shape behavior. But in part 2, we are considering the way behavior shapes belief. In liturgical parlance we say, *Lex orandi, lex credendi*, "The law of prayer is the law of belief." On this phrase, Tish Harrison Warren contends, "We come to God with our

5. Herdt, *Putting on Virtue*, 174.

little belief, however fleeting and feeble, and in prayer, we are taught to walk more deeply into truth. When my strength wanted and my words ran dry, I needed to fall into a way of belief that carried me. I needed other people's prayers."[6] Especially when we don't feel like or mean it, we need practices to help us. Behavior shapes and displays our belief in a reciprocal fashion. These monotonous routines can shape us into either more integrated and congruous selves or disintegrated and incongruous selves. The question is, Who do you want to be? And then, Who are you planning to be? If you want to grow into a person of virtue, building habits will always have the feel of inauthenticity, because it's not who you are—yet.

"IN YOUR SERVICE IS PERFECT FREEDOM"

What does it mean to be free? Paul reminds us in Galatians, "For freedom Christ has set us free" (Gal. 5:1). That sounds pretty nice. Especially in America, we love freedom. We are free from things like restraint. No one can tell us what to do or how to be. We're free. This talk of ritual seems to go right out the door.

This American concept of freedom is known as "negative freedom." It emphasizes freedom *from*. In Christianity we can say that we're free from the curse of the law. We're free from condemnation. We're free from Mosaic stipulations. We may be free *from* those regulations or guilt, but what are free *for* or free to do? We may be free from restraint, but what is the positive good we are pursuing? This deeper liberty is known as "positive freedom." G. K. Chesterton writes that "Catholic doctrine and discipline may be walls; but they are the walls of a playground."[7] The doctrines I talked about in part 1 and the habits discussed here in part 2 are not restrictive but playful. They allow us to run wild and have fun within the context of what will truly bring us joy. Rituals help us stay in eternal, flourishing, good life. God is inviting us into a fuller life with him by curbing our freedom.

In the same passage where Paul says that Christ set us free for freedom, he says, "For you were called to freedom, brothers. Only do not use your freedom as an opportunity for the flesh, but through

---

6. Warren, *Prayer in the Night*, 17.
7. Chesterton, *Orthodoxy*, 153.

love serve one another" (Gal. 5:13). This Christ-bought freedom has a positive good. We're not free to do whatever we want. That would make us slaves to ourselves and to sin. That's what Christ set us free from. In Christ we are finally free to love one another. We were unable to love others sacrificially apart from Christ.

This idea of slavery is also evident in Romans 6:15–23. In this life we don't have a choice of total freedom. The problem, to quote Bob Dylan, is that we "gotta serve somebody." Like the Israelites in Deuteronomy, we have a choice. We are either slaves of sin, which leads to death, or we are slaves of righteousness, which leads to life (Rom. 6:15–23). We get to choose our master. Which master we choose will dictate our destiny. We either earn death or receive the gift of eternal, lasting, full life.

If we are slaves of God, then every aspect of our life comes before him: our minds, hearts, and bodies. He is a master who leaves no stone unturned. He cares about it all—even our habits, even our mundane moments. Consider that the God of Israel is the Christian God. There aren't two different gods operating on two different principles. The God who made all those stipulations on how to worship is the same God we meet in the face of Jesus Christ in the New Testament. Presumably, then, God still cares about the minute details of our life. He cares about how we spend our time. He cares about what we do with our bodies. Stanley Hauerwas suggests that "any religion that does not tell you what to do with your pots and pans and genitals cannot be interesting."[8] There is no public and private divide to God. Intention and practice are not neatly divided. He cares about our doctrine and the story we inhabit, and he cares about the mundane, like pots and pans. God cares about what we do with our bodies. He cares about our habits. The content of what we worship (truth) is important, but how we worship (goodness) is just as important.

PUTTING OFF SIN: ASCETIC PRACTICES

When people expect their pastor to help them display and then heal their wounds, the Christian faith is reduced to a technique for gaining

8. Hauerwas, "Christian Practice and the Practice of Law," 750.

control over your life so you can be happy. I hope their pastor would ask, "Why would you come to me for that?"

—Stanley Hauerwas and William Willimon, "The Dangers of Providing Pastoral Care"

There's something wrong with you. I'm sorry to be so blunt, but it's true. I live with the same reality: there is something ingrained deep in the fiber of my being that is disordered. There's a gap between who I am now and who I want to become. If I didn't admit that fact, I would be a narcissist. Confessing that fact is the first step toward humility.

When Dwight Eisenhower was about ten years old, his parents gave his older brothers permission to go out trick-or-treating one Halloween. Ike, as he was called, was too young to join. Enraged by this injustice, he went into an uncontrollable frenzy. He ended up outside, punching an apple tree until his knuckles were red with blood. His father grabbed him, found a stick, and used it to spank him. Ike promptly went to bed. Later, his mother came up and found Ike crying into his pillow. She gently guided him by quoting a verse from Proverbs: "He that conquereth his own soul is greater than he who taketh a city." As she comforted him and began caring for his bloody knuckles, she warned him about the passions that waged war within him.

When Eisenhower was older, he acknowledged, "I have always looked back on that conversation as one of the most valuable moments of my life. To my youthful mind, it seemed to me that she talked for hours, but I suppose the affair was ended in fifteen or twenty minutes. At least she got me to acknowledge that I was wrong and I felt enough ease in my mind to fall asleep."[9] An earlier generation understood that we humans live in a moral drama, and central to this story is the presence of weakness and sin. In a past age, weakness was something to be reflected on and explored. Today we tend to ignore or justify weakness. We often refuse to admit we're wrong.

For Eisenhower, humility came with humiliation. As much as I hate exposure, I need to have my sin revealed if I am to know it and

9. Eisenhower, *At Ease*, 52. The verse from Proverbs quoted by his mother is a paraphrase of Prov. 16:32.

to fight against it. There is no part of this process that is pleasant. I wish there were another way, but I know no other way. Perhaps so many of us struggle with the root of sin (pride) because we never try anything worthwhile. We fear failing, so we don't fail. We play it safe and don't think about sin. We cover it up so others don't see it. Rather than try to root out sin, we ignore it. Rather than meditate, we get busy with the day. Rather than pray, we turn to our phones. As a result, we never grow in humility.

Failure is the fertilizer that makes love grow. Grace finally has a crack that it can seep through. As long as we are strong on our own, we are weak. We need to be like Paul, in whom God's "power is made perfect in weakness" (2 Cor. 12:9). The spiritual journey is painful because the false self—that self that we build up by value systems of the world to protect us from pain or emotional hurt—needs to be constantly humiliated if we are to get to the true self.[10]

This true self faces the tension of authenticity and hypocrisy. Doing good can create a feeling of wearing a mask, and being bad can feel authentic. But the redeemed self—the self the individual is in the sight of God, the self that God made that person to be—is

10. Personality tests such as Myers-Briggs, Enneagram, and StrengthsFinder, as helpful as they are in some respects, seem to be about discovering people's "true selves" without reference to God. I may not go so far as to say they are bad. I find them interesting and have been helped by all three. However, I do think they have limits. The discovery of ourselves is meant to happen in and through conversation with Christ rather than through independent studies of personality data. In Christian spirituality the goal is to know ourselves more reliably and to root out sin more extensively.

My hesitation is that personality tests can become an excuse for vice. I think we should be critical in our evaluation of our own sin and gracious in our evaluation of others'. I think we often get that reversed. We are typically gracious in regard to our own sin. "I'm a little off-putting and harsh with those around me, because I'm a 1." Or "I'm an INTJ, so I don't really trust authorities." But then, just as quickly as we excuse our own sin, we judge others' sin. Since I'm an introvert, I can look at extroverts and think, *They just want to be the center of attention. What vanity.* Meanwhile, I think of myself as a refined introvert, as someone who's thoughtful and reserved. I am not inclined to ask whether I just don't love people enough to go out of my comfort zone to talk to them. It must be someone else's problem. Rather than use our understanding of ourselves to fight sin, we use it as an excuse for sin. This is not to say we all need to be bubbly people or there's some overall standard of sanctification. Yet within our unique personality, we should become comfortable with the way God made us but ruthlessly root out sin where it's present.

their deepest, truest self. Discovering this self requires the false self to die. And death is hard.

Ascetic practices help us die. Asceticism is a way of curbing the false self and living into the true self. The goal, to borrow a statement from John the Baptist, is for us to decrease and for Jesus to increase (John 3:30). The monastics urge fellow believers to die to self for the sake of life with Christ. A written tradition started with Evagrius and developed over the years through John Cassian, Saint Gregory the Great, Saint Augustine, Saint Thomas Aquinas, and the poet Dante. It has a rich lineage. Instead of finding their strengths, they sought out their weaknesses, or what they termed vices. There were seven vices: envy, vainglory, sloth, avarice, anger, gluttony, and lust. Pride was the root of all of these. Vices were not one-off acts but, rather, were patterns of behavior that marked the monastics.

Have you ever been telling someone a problem and they attempt to define the problem in their own words? Sometimes they can't quite relate, or the message you're trying to communicate and the message they're receiving are different. But other times, a friend listens and understands and rephrases the issue better than you explained it. So you respond, "Yes! That's it. That's what I'm going through." The great tradition dealing with vice does something like this for us. It names the soul struggle we feel and makes us feel a bit less alone, a bit less strange and alienated from the history of saints before us. And not only does it name the struggle, but it provides help and counsel.

Each of these vices takes a good thing and twists it. Gluttony is the desire for food twisted to abstinence from food for unhealthy weight goals or indulgence in food without regard for others. Lust is the desire for sex twisted to the self so that it is about merely being pleased rather than loving. The remedy for all the vices is properly ordered love; it is loving the good in the right way.

Saint Isaac the Syrian wrote, "Blessed is the man who knows his weakness. This knowledge becomes for him the foundation and the beginning of his coming unto all good and beautiful things."[11] The goal is not to "find ourselves" or to judge other people. Rather, it is to

---

11. Isaac the Syrian, *Mystic Treatises*, chap. 8, "What Is It That Helps a Man to Come Near unto God?" (Wensinck, 70).

discover what moral weaknesses we need to root out. The purpose of this list is not to overwhelm us with guilt. But like a personality test, these vices are listed to help us identify a disorder we may be prone to. Knowing that disorder, we can begin to habituate ourselves to a virtuous life by putting off the vicious life. We all will likely identify with more than one or two vices. As I review the list, it's hard to pick just one vice that I need to address. However, it's impossible to make all improvements at once. Start with the vice that rings most true, or ask which vice has the strongest hold. Which would be hardest to fight? Pray and ask God for guidance. Seek the advice of mentors about which vice(s) they see in you. Then fight like hell—because living a vice-laden life leads there.

One of the ways to battle sin is asceticism. The word comes from the Greek *askeō*, which means "to train or exercise." Ascetic practices are a system of restraints that allow us to work at conquering our passions rather than letting our passions conquer our soul. Former archbishop of Canterbury Rowan Williams describes the ascetic as one "called to keep on knocking at the door of Christ's internal dwelling—the natural intelligence within us that is being restored by the Spirit's grace. . . . What we aim at is not perfect keeping of the commandments as some sort of human achievement, but the freedom to receive the gift of Christ being formed in us and to guard it by means of our watchfulness."[12] Sometimes we limit our freedom and say no to a desire so we can attain a good beyond immediate pleasure. Asceticism helps us through this delaying of gratification. By fasting from food or screens or noise, we long for Jesus in the way we would long for food or screens or noise. These practices turn us from the love of created things to the love of the Creator. And as John Cassian reminds his followers, the idea is not merely to do the practice for the sake of doing something hard. He insists,

> This harsh struggle has to be fought in both body and soul. . . . Bodily fasting is not enough to bring about perfect self-restraint and true purity; it must be accompanied by contrition of heart, intense prayer to God, frequent meditation on the Scriptures, toil and manual labour. . . . Humility of soul helps more than everything else. . . . We should

12. Williams, *Looking East in Winter*, 31–32.

not trust in our own strength and ascetic practice, but in the help of our Master, God, . . . for such a victory is beyond man's natural powers.[13]

Again, the goal is grace-driven effort rooted in the gospel, not a self-righteousness that leads to pride. The whole of the Christian life requires dependence.

Asceticism is not a rejection of creation as bad or the material world as evil. Rather, as rapper Tobe Nwigwe puts it, "It's hard to get your gift from God when both your hands is full."[14] Asceticism helps pry our hands from the good things of the world for the greater good beyond the good world. Saint Basil of Caesarea describes renunciation as "the transference of the human heart to a heavenly mode of life, so that we can say: 'But our conversation is in heaven.' Also . . . it is the first step toward the likeness to Christ, who, being rich, became poor for our sake."[15] In his earthly ministry, Christ had access to the material world but at times renounced the good creation for a greater good, like when he was tempted by the devil in the wilderness. The material world is loved by God and should be by Christians as well. The goal of carrying out ascetic practices is to reject our sinful passions and see the world as beautiful so we can heal it and be reconciled with it. Vices distort our vision of the good creation, and therefore vices need to be removed.

PUTTING ON CHRIST: THE POWER OF HABITS

A few years ago I began training for a triathlon with my high school soccer coach. We had run a couple of marathons together, so I felt pretty good about the running part. And I had gotten into biking after college, so that wasn't an issue. How difficult could swimming be?

As it turns out, very difficult! Without the proper form, I put in a lot of effort. I tried, and I tried, and I tried. I exhausted myself with trying. During training I hopped in the pool, pushed off the wall, and began my stroke. I swam for as long as I could—it seemed like

13. Cassian, *Conferences*, 75.
14. Nwigwe, "I CHOOSE YOU."
15. Basil, *Ascetical Works*, 256.

hours. Finally, out of breath, I popped my head out of the water and looked at my watch: two minutes and thirty seconds had gone by. I lasted about two laps before I had to take a break, or else I'd have drowned. Something wasn't working. I needed a fix.

For me, swimming was not a matter of effort. I was trying hard. I put everything into it. But there's a difference between training and trying. Training is done with intention and purpose. Even with the right goal, I needed to change the means of practice. So, like a good modern pragmatist, I went to YouTube. I watched video after video of long-distance swim form. I tried different exercises. I asked my soccer coach, who grew up swimming, for help. He looked at my form and helped me learn how a good swim stroke felt as opposed to an inefficient one. Slowly but surely, two laps turned into eight, and eight into sixteen, and sixteen to forty. Eventually, I could swim the required 1.2 miles. Getting to this point required intentional training beyond mere trying. It was the result of dedicatedly practicing habits for months in order to unlearn a bad habit.

I needed more than knowledge or intention in order to be a good swimmer. I needed the practice. I could intend to be a good swimmer, but if I never showed up for laps, my intention wouldn't matter. I could read all about swimming and know the best swimmers, but unless I practiced, I would not be a good swimmer. I needed help seeing what a good swimmer does as opposed to what a bad swimmer does. The same rings true for any other activity. It's not enough to read a textbook on being a good soccer player or piano player or knitter. No one will arrive at excellence by thinking about an activity.

Take the example of Michael Phelps. The decorated Olympian swimmer didn't wake up one day and become a world champion by surprise. His achievements required him to curb his freedom. His choice of who he wanted to be limited his freedom. He could not do whatever he wanted. He limited himself from enjoying late nights so he could perform at a high level early in the morning. He limited his diet to nutritious calories (and lots of them) to fuel his demanding training. He did what he did not "want" to do in order to become the person he truly wanted to become. He maintained a boring schedule of routine and rhythm to arrive at excellence.

The same principle is at work in spiritual formation. I can't say that I'm mature simply because I read about what other mature people did. I can't say I'm spiritually formed by knowing a lot. If I am to grow, practices and habits must accompany what I say. Habits help us "put on" Christ to be slowly trained in becoming like him. In other words, habits are as formative as they are expressive. They are not merely actions we do; they do something *to us*. Stanley Hauerwas opines that "there's much to be said for Christianity as repetition and I think evangelicalism doesn't have enough repetition in a way that will form Christians to survive in a world that constantly tempts us to always think we have to do something new."[16] Repetition, habits, and rituals train us. They are the means of grace by which we train ourselves for godliness (1 Tim. 4:7). Praying together with a unified voice is not merely something we do; it forms and unifies a group together. Reverencing or kneeling to pray isn't mere expression; it's training us in a posture, affecting us by what we do.

I love the way Frederick Buechner ties ritual with sacrament: "A ritual is the ceremonial acting out of the profane in order to show forth its sacredness. A sacrament is the breaking through of the sacred into the profane. A sacrament is God offering his holiness to us. A ritual is our raising up the holiness of our humanity to God."[17] A ritual is the reverse order of a sacrament. In a sacrament, God bestows holiness to the ordinary. In a ritual, we offer something ordinary to the sacred. There's something dignifying and holy about ritual.

Tish Harrison Warren shows that everyone has rituals that guide their lives. She writes, "Examining my daily liturgy *as a liturgy*—as something that both revealed and shaped what I love and worship—allowed me to realize that my daily practices were malforming, making me less alive, less human, less able to give and receive love throughout my day."[18] Our desires are shaped by what we repeat. Habits and rituals cultivate certain dispositions, what one is prone to do. They develop our character. If we intentionally develop good and constructive habits, they will harden into compulsion, and we will

16. Mohler, "Nearing the End."
17. Buechner, *Wishful Thinking*, 99.
18. Warren, *Liturgy of the Ordinary*, 31.

want to do the good we know to do. It will be who we are without even thinking about it.

In Aristotelian philosophy, one acquires virtue by acting like one already has it. Michael Phelps turned into an Olympic champion by acting like he was one. We grow in virtue by acting like we are virtuous.

In baptism a clear and amazing reality is affirmed: "This is my beloved child, with whom I am well pleased." Before you do anything good or bad, God loves you. You are favored. You are righteous. God gives you virtue. And the Christian life is living into our baptism, living into the reality that the old self is dead and the new life "is hidden with Christ" (Col. 3:3). You may feel that sin is strong and Christ is weak, but that's not what baptism says. The blood of Christ, which washes away sin, is as sure as the water that washes over you. Your state before God is one of a beloved child. This reality may not seem real. It may not "fit" yet, but this is who you are. You may not feel Christlike, but that's your new nature. Acting like Christ is not pretending but is, rather, the very means of becoming who you are in Christ. In his well-known book *Mere Christianity*, C. S. Lewis insists, "When you are behaving as if you loved someone, you will presently come to love him. If you injure someone you dislike, you will find yourself disliking him more. If you do him a good turn, you will find yourself disliking him less."[19] In other words, there is virtue in going through the motions at times. We often think change happens from the inside out, that our thoughts dictate our actions. Once we have better reasons, then we will make a change. But often the exact opposite is true. Our actions shape our motives.

We can expect that the habits of virtue will be both natural and unnatural. Loving people is natural in the sense that we all want to be loved and treated kindly. It's second nature to desire love. However, it's unnatural at the same time, because love is the hardest thing to do—doing the unselfish thing rather than the selfish thing, putting the needs of others above our own. We need help refining the unnatural desires and becoming naturally good. Habits help. They can be seen as the guardrails or custodians of love.

19. Lewis, *Mere Christianity*, 131.

Let me give an example of how habits shape who we become. I officiated my first wedding when I was twenty-two years old. My friends were set to be married at a beautiful outdoor location in northeast Ohio. (Yes, beautiful places exist in northeast Ohio.) Since this was my first time officiating a wedding, I had no idea what I was doing, so I received a lot of advice from mentors and pastors. One of the pieces of wisdom that I passed on to the groomsmen during the rehearsal dinner was "Do *not* lock your knees." When people lock their legs, it creates some circulation problems, and they may pass out. For groomsmen, passing out during the wedding ceremony is typically frowned upon.

The day of the wedding arrived, and it was a perfect Ohio summer day. The ceremony was conducted beside a small pond, close to an outdoor reception area shaded by a decorated pavilion. I led the groomsmen out. We watched as the bridesmaids walked down the aisle. The big reveal of the bride went swimmingly, everyone standing. The bride's family gave her away, and I began, "Dearly beloved, we are gathered here today . . ." I was waxing eloquent about the meaning and beauty of marriage, how it reminds us of the love that binds us together and, most important, of the love that God has for us, his church. Then *bang!* Man down.

The younger brother of the bride was on the ground. He thought I said, "*Do* lock your knees." Before I could react, the groom's dad sprang into action. I knew him to be one of the most selfless men I had ever met. He woke up before everyone else to deliver papers to provide for his family. He did hard physical labor during the day. As soon as he walked through the doorway into his home, he knew what needed doing to help his wife and large Italian family. I never saw him complain. I never saw him without a smile. He's one of those people I want to be.

In this moment of crisis, my friend's dad was habituated to act. He was in the habit of helping, so he did the natural thing. He didn't consider the options or do a cost analysis. He rose to action.

I, on the other hand, froze. I didn't know what to do. *This was not covered in seminary. No one taught me this. Do I help? Do I go on? Do I make a joke? What kind of joke is appropriate?* I sat there stunned, not unwilling to help but not knowing what to do. Unlike

Anthony's dad, I was not the kind of person who knew what to do. Life came calling, and he responded without a second thought. Life revealed who we really were in that moment. I was stunned and stuck. He sprang to help without balking.

The goal of formation is not an unthoughtful or an unthinking faith. Anthony's dad had been formed in such a way that his most natural reaction was to assist. He likely didn't think about it in the moment, but I'm sure he had been formed to think about what the death of Christ meant for his life, to consider how Jesus's sacrifice motivates our sacrifice for others, to understand how Jesus's life of servitude ought to shape his life of servitude. The reasons to act weren't absent, but he didn't need reasons in the moment. Reasons had shaped his habits, which in turn shaped who he was in that moment.

In the medieval period there was a distinction between formed and unformed faith. Theologian Ellen Charry explains: "What Thomas [Aquinas] called formed faith corresponds to what for us is reflective prayer, study, and service, while unformed faith corresponds to dutiful prayer and service. One should not shun beginning with dutiful practices, for these are the elementary levels of Christian training. But once one yearns for God, mindless practices will not do."[20] The goal is not to go through life unreflectively, though beginners may not yet understand the practices fully. In the wedding example, I realized that I had all the reasons and theology required for action, yet a man with less theological training actually did something. I needed training in dutiful practice to allow my rituals to catch up with my ideas. As in the Lord's Supper, meaning grows as I practice. The intention becomes more meaningful as I act and as God acts upon me.

CONCLUSION

In *The Great Divorce*, C. S. Lewis depicts the afterlife. A man who has died is walking around heaven to see if he wants to stay. One of my favorite passages in the book explores the question, How much do we really want to be rid of sin? Or in other words, How badly do we want to be virtuous?

20. Charry, *By the Renewing of Your Minds*, 242.

This recently deceased wanderer overhears a conversation between a fellow ghost and what he realizes is an angel. The ghost has a lizard on his shoulder, whispering to him. The angel wants to kill it, but the ghost goes through a series of excuses. He'll get a second opinion. The lizard said it would behave. The ghost isn't feeling very well anyway, so maybe tomorrow. Is killing it really necessary? The passage is reminiscent of Augustine's conversion scene. "Get rid of us, forever? . . . Tomorrow is better."

The ghost talks about the lizard the way we usually think of our tendencies to sin. God may need to tweak us a little bit, we tell ourselves. He may need to give some direction but not *change* us. He doesn't want us to be that radical or extreme with sin. Ridding our life of sin shouldn't hurt. God just helps us behave a little better and intervenes when we need his assistance with an urgent matter. But he doesn't want to press us.

The lizard pleads its case as the angel threatens to kill it. The lizard, aware of the angel's power, promises to be good. He may have gone too far in the past but not anymore.

The angel asks for permission to kill the lizard. "I know it will kill me," the ghost says. The story continues:

> "It won't. But supposing it did?"
> "You're right. It would be better to be dead than to live with this creature."
> "Then I may?"
> "Damn and blast you! Go on, can't you? Get it over. Do what you like," bellowed the Ghost: but ended, whimpering, "God help me. God help me."

> In the next moment the Ghost gave a scream of agony such as I never heard on Earth. The Burning One closed his crimson grip on the reptile: twisted it, while it bit and writhed, and then flung it, broken-backed, on the turf.[21]

Do we care to get rid of our vices like this? Even when it hurts? Even when it costs us something? Even if it kills us? Or are we comfortable just to quiet sin for a while, to let it talk us into keeping it around?

21. Lewis, *Great Divorce*, 351.

How serious are we about putting off sin and putting on Christ (see Rom. 13:14)?

Here's the beautiful thing about God and the reason we don't have to hide our vice from him: "He is faithful and just to forgive us" (1 John 1:9). All God requires is that we be honest with ourselves and say, "God, you are right about the state of my heart. Woe is me." The purging of sin does not consist of us cleaning ourselves up. It does not come from us. God is faithful, trustworthy, able, reliable to deal with our sin. And he is just; he takes the payment he requires. On the cross, God is seen as both *just*—the consequence of sin is death (Rom. 6:23)—and *justifier*—all who call on the Lord will be saved (Joel 2:32; Rom. 10:13).

This is the gospel. And it's why we can freely bring sin into light without fear of judgment. The judgment has already been delivered. The purging is paid. We have confidence to approach God, to say, "Here I am," and to know God as a Father who doesn't dole out punishment but who extends his arms in welcome. We can live a good life, an eternal life.

✳ 6 ✳

DOROTHY DAY

WE MUST LOVE ONE ANOTHER OR DIE

As you survey your life, what would you point to as most formative? When was a time you grew the most?

I've recently begun to put this question to some friends and students. It has been interesting to hear how people respond.

Some mention an experience based on an activity—maybe a mission trip or a discipleship relationship. But the most common answer I receive is a time of intense suffering. Most people wouldn't wish such an experience on their worst enemies, yet these moments, events, or periods are the things that made them who they are. They have been the most spiritually formative.

I sure wish that weren't the case. But I know it's true for me. The most soul-shaping times were the times when God felt the most distant. God was actually closest when he seemed furthest away.

This idea puts us in direct confrontation with our age of authenticity. Authenticity is "the notion that each of us has an original way of being human" and that "each of us has to discover what it is to be ourselves."[1] It's rooted in expressive individualism, which says people's feelings dictate their lives. God wouldn't conflict with people's

1. Taylor, *Ethics of Authenticity*, 61.

feelings, right? Reality is oriented around how people feel. But if God shapes us in suffering, then maybe our feelings aren't that dependable. Maybe an authentic life means conforming not to our feelings but to the image of God.

Suffering forces us to become acquainted with ourselves. There's no way to hide from pain. This confrontation with pain forces upon us a realization of how much of life is out of our control and how utterly dependent we are. This knowledge shatters our illusions of power. Suffering also allows us to comfort others (2 Cor. 1:3–7) with a sense of deep gratitude. It is not that we are thankful for the suffering we have experienced; this reaction would trivialize suffering. Yet there's a sense that the suffering shapes us to become deeper people, more whole and holy people.

A podcast called *The Rise and Fall of Mars Hill* documents the rise to fame and then the fall from grace of a pastor in Seattle named Mark Driscoll. One of the most powerful lines for me came in a late episode. One of the members of the church was describing why his dad didn't like Driscoll. He said, "Mark Driscoll is a harsh man. He doesn't understand mercy. And he doesn't understand mercy because he hasn't suffered."[2] I heard that while driving to work, and I broke down and wept. For maybe the first time, I was grateful for my suffering. Don't get me wrong: I don't want to go through it again! Yet as I looked back on my life, I was profoundly thankful for the suffering that shaped me. The comedian Stephen Colbert once expressed the same sentiment. Referring to the grief of losing his father and two brothers when he was young, he declared that he had learned to love the things that he most wished hadn't happened, saying, "What punishments of God are not gifts?"[3]

What I have just said in the preceding paragraph invites a reconsideration of one's own spiritual autobiography. Perhaps we should rethink how and when God is at work. God may be closest when we think he's furthest. He may be closer than you think when you feel like he's absent.

2. "Aftermath," *The Rise and Fall of Mars Hill* (podcast), 1:23:55.
3. Anderson Cooper, "Stephen Colbert: Grateful for Grief," *All There Is*, Sept. 21, 2022, 3:00, https://www.cnn.com/audio/podcasts/all-there-is-with-anderson-cooper/episodes/ae2f9ebb-1bc6-4d47-b0f0-af17008dcd0c.

DOROTHY DAY: A SUFFERING SAINT

One woman's life confirms the formative shape of suffering. By "showing up" in regular and mundane ways, she found herself transformed. Dorothy Day allowed pain to shape her.

If you want to live an easy life, don't read Dorothy Day. Skip this chapter. But if you want to live an easy life, Day would likely remind you, then don't read the Bible either.

The title of her autobiography is *The Long Loneliness*. But in her loneliness, she wasn't alone. She lived a life with God by choosing to love, even when it felt like loneliness. The line is a quote from a nun named Mary Ward: "I think, dear child, the trouble and the long loneliness you hear me speak of is not far from me, which whensoever it is, happy success will follow. . . . The pain is great, but very endurable, because He who lays on the burden also carries it."[4] The thing about suffering that makes it bearable is that God is with us in it. He helps carry the load. He is walking with us when we limp along.

Day starts her autobiography with an explanation of confession, which places her in line with Saint Augustine. She is confessing her life and faith and confessing her sins, "not the sins of others, or your own virtues, but only your ugly, gray, drab, monotonous sins."[5] She is acquainted with her true self because she is acquainted with the humiliation that accompanies humility. She does not ignore or hide her sins but brings them into the open to be forgiven and healed.

Dorothy Day begins by confessing that she did not have a saintly start. Growing up in the early 1900s, she was haunted by God but not yet rescued. She was born into an Episcopal family, yet there wasn't much religious practice or conversation. It was not necessarily the truthfulness of God that exposed her to Christianity; rather, the relationships that God weaved into her upbringing showed her Christian life. There were people like a friend in Oakland named Birdie or a mentor named Mrs. Barrett, whom she saw kneeling. "This posture, this gesture, convinced me that worship, adoration, thanksgiving, supplication—these were the noblest acts of which men were capable

4. Day, *Long Loneliness*, epigraph.
5. Day, *Long Loneliness*, 10.

in this life."[6] So, when she and her sister were growing up, they would, at Dorothy's prompting, "practice being saints."[7]

This practicing of sainthood was formative, but faith didn't "take" during her early life—at least not in a conscious way. There were several precursors to transformation in her life. Day's religious life came in fits and starts, like a motor than won't quite turn over. Once, she was arrested for protesting and found herself at the proverbial rock bottom, sitting in a jail cell. Day asked for a Bible on the second day, and she "read it with the sense of coming back to something of my childhood that I had lost. My heart swelled with joy and thankfulness for the Psalms."[8] Yet, as much as she clung to the Bible for comfort in this time, her socialist sensibilities led her to see religion as, in the oft-repeated phrase, an "opiate of the masses," a sort of pill to quell the cries of the exploited. Moreover, she didn't want to come to Jesus in weakness. As she describes it, "I did not want to go to God in defeat and sorrow. I did not want to depend on Him. I was like the child that wants to walk by itself, I kept brushing away the hand that held me up."[9] She was attracted to the person and ethic of Jesus but became convinced that radical care for the poor was not meek like Jesus taught. Governmental policy and radical protest were the ways to change.

Day describes several conversions in her life, as Augustine does, and most formative for her was a conversion to the poor. While living in Chicago as a youth, she read *The Jungle* by Upton Sinclair, which fictionally but realistically displays the grotesque and awful working conditions of industrial workers in Chicago. She couldn't look at the world the same. "I had received a call, a vocation, a direction to my life," Day writes.[10] Despite Jesus's regular injunctions to care for the downcast and "least of these" (Matt. 25:40), she noticed that precious few Christians cared for the poor. Day saw them as too concerned with "pie in the sky" spirituality rather than the practical call to care for material needs on earth. So, she joined the Socialist

6. Day, *Long Loneliness*, 107.
7. Day, *Long Loneliness*, 25.
8. Day, *Long Loneliness*, 80.
9. Day, *Long Loneliness*, 81.
10. Day, *Long Loneliness*, 38.

Party. There, Day found her people and had an awakening with deep Christian sensibilities.

Day writes of her coming of age that "my freedom intoxicated me."[11] In New York City, she was involved with the Greenwich intellectuals, an avant-garde and free-spirited group that was involved in all sorts of debauchery—legendary drug use, sexual experimentation, and other countercultural activities. It was said that even in this crowd Dorothy could drink her companions under the table—a fact that, if mentioned after her conversion, would bring out her anger. She didn't like to talk about her life before Jesus. She fell in love, got pregnant, had an abortion, and attempted suicide on two occasions. Her freedom may have been intoxicating, but it was a freedom leading her to death. She experienced the slavery that comes with negative freedom.

SEEDS OF CONVERSION

The catalyst for Day's transformation was a baby. She became pregnant again by a man named Forster, with whom she was in a common-law marriage. Forster had no interest in traditional morals or commitments. He didn't want to be a father, but Day wanted to be a mother. So, she kept the baby this time. In the days leading up to the birth, she was in regular prayer. She believed religion to be an opiate of the masses yet was praying not out of desperation but out of joy. She was praying not to soothe her unhappiness but because she had found a kind of happiness.

Then the moment of birth transformed her. Birthing her daughter, Tamar Teresa, generated a thankfulness she couldn't account for. Who could she be thankful to? Mother Earth? The universe? These weren't sufficient answers. One can't be thankful to impersonal forces.

In her hospital room, days after giving birth, she wrote an article for a communist magazine called *The Masses* to explain her incredible joy. Reflecting on the experience, she acknowledged, "If I had written the greatest book, composed the greatest symphony, painted

11. Day, *Long Loneliness*, 44.

the most beautiful painting or carved the most exquisite figure, I could not have felt the more exalted creator than I did when they placed my child in my arms. . . . No human creature could receive or contain so vast a flood of love and joy as I often felt after the birth of my child. With this came the need to worship, to adore."[12] Day realized that in her gratitude there had to be a personal being to be thankful to. So she started going to Mass regularly on Sunday mornings. Tamar was baptized, and not long after, Dorothy joined her daughter in the Catholic Church.

COMMITMENT TO THE CHURCH

Dorothy Day had a fraught relationship with the church from the very beginning, yet she continued to love the ecclesial community—"not for itself," she insists, "because it is so often a scandal to me. Romano Guardini said the Church is the Cross on which Christ was crucified; one could not separate Christ from His Cross, and one must live in a state of permanent dissatisfaction with the Church."[13] Day lived with that dissatisfaction.

From the beginning, joining the church required sacrifice. She was in an illicit relationship with Forster, and he had no interest in religious life. Joining was no easy decision. Commitment to the church would "mean facing a life alone and I clung to family life. It was hard to contemplate giving up a mate in order that my child and I could become members of the Church."[14] She went about her participation "grimly, coldly, making acts of faith, and certainly with no consolation whatsoever."[15] She doubted. She wrestled. Was Christianity supposed to feel so cold? Could it require this much sacrifice? When do the emotions catch up? To start, Day went through the motions. To continue, she found the value of routine, especially daily Mass. She asserts, "Without the sacraments of the church, primarily the Eucharist, the Lord's Supper, as it is called, I certainly do not think I could go on. . . . I do not always approach it from need, or with joy

12. Roberts, *Dorothy Day and the* Catholic Worker, 47.
13. Day, *Long Loneliness*, 150.
14. Day, *Long Loneliness*, 137.
15. Day, *Long Loneliness*, 148.

and thanksgiving. After 38 years of almost daily communion, one can confess to a routine, but it is like the routine of taking daily food."[16] In a recent commentary on routine and liturgy, Tish Harrison Warren compares the Eucharist to eating leftovers.[17] Most people cannot remember what they ate for lunch last Tuesday. It was likely not a life-changing experience. However, these forgettable meals are what sustain us. They transform us—slowly and without notice or fanfare. Daily routines are like that. They are small and unremarkable, yet they make a significant difference.

Day saw these ordinary, eucharistic acts as hope for the poor. Reflecting on Day, Timothy O'Malley writes, "Most of all, she knew that the presence of the flesh and blood poor, the scandal of social injustice, was a Eucharistic problem. She celebrated the Liturgy of the Hours and the Eucharistic liturgy each day. She spent time in adoration before the Eucharistic Lord. From the Eucharist, from the grace she received, she became an accidental icon of love for all those who knew her."[18] The Eucharist is a symbol of incarnation to the poor. It is a picture of Philippians 2 love, which comes down to us. Day's commitment to the church allowed her to love the poor in tangible and deep ways. The habit of adoration allowed her to see things that she could otherwise not see and to become a person she could otherwise not become. The church and the poor were in tension for Day, but she could not reject either.

COMMITMENT TO THE POOR

After Day joined the church, the next big move in her life journey was meeting Peter Maurin. A third of her autobiography is about her relationship with Maurin, who was the cofounder of the *Catholic Worker*. Maurin was an eccentric and aloof intellectual who desired to form a society and culture in which it was easier for people to be good. "He wanted them to stretch out their arms to their brothers, because he knew that the surest way to find God, to find the good,

---

16. Day, *Duty of Delight*, 519.
17. Warren, *Liturgy of the Ordinary*, 61–73.
18. O'Malley, "Why Americans Struggle to Understand Catholicism."

was through one's brother."[19] This program was to cultivate an imagination of seeing and loving Christ in the other and especially in the poor, the naked, the sick, and the hungry.

Day's conversion to Christianity only sharpened her social conscience, prodding her to a deeper commitment to the poor of the world. She was not merely caring for the exploited by talking about it or sharing ideas, but now she had deeper reasons for caring for the impoverished. She did not merely march or picket or organize or give. To adequately love the poor, "one must live with them, share with their suffering, too. Give up one's privacy, and mental and spiritual comforts as well as physical."[20] Christ incarnates himself on earth—he gets in the messy details of our daily lives. If we desire to love the world as Christ did, then Day instructs us to live among those we are called to love. She was a love warrior, and she invites us into such an eternal life.

Day and Maurin were driven by a philosophy of personalism. In a culture that wants to change the world, personalism insists on starting with small acts of love for the person closest to oneself.

Being a virtuous person starts with the immediate community. Personalism asks how people treat their moms and dads, their roommates, their spouses and children. David Brooks comments, "Personalism holds that we each have a deep personal obligation to live simply, to look after the needs of our brothers and sisters, and to share in the happiness and misery they are suffering. The personalist brings his whole person to serve another whole person."[21] The Catholic Worker movement exemplified such values. There were no "deserving poor" and "undeserving poor." There were the poor, and Christians were called to care for the vulnerable among them.

To be sure, Day was no idealist. She lived in the difficult tensions of caring for the vulnerable, to the ire and dismay even of her colleagues. When young people would come to volunteer at her soup kitchen, she would inform them, "There are two things you need to know about poor people: they are ungrateful, and they smell."[22] In

19. Day, *Long Loneliness*, 171.
20. Day, *Long Loneliness*, 214.
21. Brooks, *Road to Character*, 90.
22. As told by Bishop Robert Barron in *The Strangest Way*, 152.

modern terms, service is not fit for Instagram. Mercy is not for likes or clicks. It won't make you feel good. But it is our duty, and we are called to such a life of love.

Day asked what kind of people we are meant to be and worked hard to help others achieve that virtue. She shared Maurin's goal of cultivating a community in which it was easier for people to be good. Referring to the issue of abortion, Myles Werntz summarizes Day's philosophy this way: "And so Day's consistent approach to abortion can be summed up in this way: if you want a law to be undone, make it meaningless to have it. Rather than try to legislate it out of existence, cultivate a world in which abortion is unthinkable because of the love we share with one another, and—when pregnancies happen unwanted—make it possible for children to be received into loving communities."[23] Day was motivated by the law of love rather than the laws of the land. She wanted to cultivate a community in which vice becomes increasingly unthinkable, where we don't need laws to regulate virtue. Of course, we will need laws to guide us when our flesh is weak, but if we took the law of love seriously, laws would become extraneous. We would begin to act with our neighbors' best interests in mind.

Referring to Jesus's miracle of multiplication, "loaves and fishes" was a phrase Dorothy repeated from Peter Maurin. As D. L. May-field writes, Dorothy knew that "both came through prayer and also pounding the pavement."[24] She followed the wisdom of ritual in Philippians 2:12–13. She worked out her faith "with fear and trembling" (pounding the pavement), knowing it was God who was working in her (prayer). Loaves and fishes, indeed. It's all we have.

CONCLUSION

Day lived a remarkable life. She believed in obedience and submission to the church even though the church frustrated her. She loved the poor till the end. Day also ended up on the FBI watchlist for addressing the moral issues of her day: from speaking against

---

23. Werntz, "Making Little of the Law and Everything of Love."
24. Mayfield, *Unruly Saint*, 130.

Japanese internment camps to burning military draft cards to protesting nuclear bombs to advocating for racial justice. She was an equal-opportunity offender. She wasn't safe, but she lived a life of goodness.

In her autobiography Day writes, "Faith that works through love is the mark of the supernatural life. God always gives us a chance to show our preference for Him. With Abraham it was to sacrifice his only son. With me it was to give up my married life with Forster. You do these things blindly, not because of your natural inclination—you are going against nature when you do them—but because you wish to live in conformity with the will of God."[25] And Day saw the importance of ritual for living in conformity with God. "Ritual, how could we do without it!"[26] She compares ritual to a husband unthinkingly and unreflectively kissing his wife before leaving for work. "That kiss on occasion turns to rapture, a burning fire of tenderness and love. And with this to stay her she demands the 'ritual' of affection shown. . . . We have too little ritual in our lives."[27] Day knows the power of practice. She knows that love thrives with habits.

In the moments when we feel most disconnected, when we feel that we need church the least, when it's hard to enter the church's doors, showing up is the first step toward grace. Even when—especially when—she didn't feel like it, Day came to church out of duty. She showed up. And through the fulfillment of her duty, she was transformed.

Currently, Dorothy Day is in the long process of being canonized, or "sainted." Eventually, she may be Saint Dorothy. She wouldn't have liked it. To be a saint, according to her, is to not be taken seriously. It puts her life out of reach—"Well, of course she can do it, since she's a saint. But I can't. I'm 'normal.'" Ironically, perhaps that mentality of Day's, that reluctance to be a saint, is what makes her fit for sainthood. Righteousness without self-righteousness.

---

25. Day, *Long Loneliness*, 256.
26. Day, *Long Loneliness*, 199.
27. Day, *Long Loneliness*, 200.

PRACTICES

CREATE A RULE OF LIFE

"Rule" does not carry its usual meaning here. It refers to a pattern. Based on the goal or vision of who you want to be, what habits can get you there? With a mentor, it can be very helpful to plan daily, weekly, monthly, seasonal, and annual patterns. What things do you want to commit to every day, every week, every season, every year? You can divide your life into different categories: vocational, relational, familial, spiritual, bodily. Completing this process with a mentor or spiritual director can be a helpful way to keep you accountable as well. Remember: start small. Keep things manageable instead of trying to do everything right from the beginning. You can add more later. Be realistic.

FASTING

Fasting helps us long for God, as mentioned in chapter 5, and it reveals the way we depend on created things rather than the Creator. There's nothing sinful about food or social media or cellphone use or sleep, yet by prying our hands off these good gifts, we open ourselves up. Fasting empties the self so it can receive more of God.

SELF-EXAMINATION

There's an Ignatian practice called "examen," in which the participant reviews their day in the presence of God, looking for consolations and desolations. Where did God seem present in a way that brought joy, comfort, and peace? What things during the day made the person feel drained, sorrowful, or angry? This regular practice of reflecting on the day, acknowledging where God was, can be a helpful practice for both gratitude and repentance.

SERVICE

Service is a great formative practice that helps us love our neighbor. Sometimes, acting the part shapes us to enjoy the part. A regular rhythm of serving neighbors—whether through a block party, regular hospitality, or service at a soup kitchen or homeless shelter—can help us love God by loving our neighbor. All spiritual formation that forms us vertically, with God, has horizontal implications with our neighbors.[28]

RESOURCES

Baldwin, James. *Go Tell It on the Mountain*. New York: Vintage, 2013.

Cassian, John. *The Conferences*. Translated by Colm Luibheid. New York: Paulist Press, 1985.

Herdt, Jennifer. *Putting on Virtue: The Legacy of the Splendid Vices*. Chicago: University of Chicago Press, 2008.

Mattison, William, III. *Introducing Moral Theology: True Happiness and the Virtues*. Grand Rapids: Brazos, 2008.

28. See Bennett, *Practices of Love*.

PART 3

BEAUTY

THE CONTEMPLATIVE LIFE

Only wonder comprehends anything. . . . Wonder makes us fall to our knees.

—attributed to Gregory of Nyssa

One thing have I asked of the LORD,
    that will I seek after:
that I may dwell in the house of the LORD
    all the days of my life,
to gaze upon the beauty of the LORD
    and to inquire in his temple.

—Psalm 27:4

Perseverance—yes, more and more one sees that it is the great thing. But there is a thing that must not be overlooked. Perseverance is not hanging on to some course which we have set our minds to, and refusing to let go. It is not even a matter of getting a bulldog grip on the faith and not letting the devil pry us loose from it—though many of the saints made it look that way. Really, there is something lacking in such a hope as that. Hope is a greater scandal than we think. I am coming to think that God . . . loves and helps best those who are so beat and have so much nothing when they come to die that it is almost as if they had persevered in nothing but had gradually lost everything, piece by piece, until there was nothing left but God. Hence perseverance is not hanging on but letting go. That of course is terrible.

—Thomas Merton, letter to Dorothy Day

❉ 7 ❉

The BEATIFIC VISION

BECOMING WHAT YOU BEHOLD

Every face has beauty, but none is beauty itself. Your face, O Lord, has beauty, and this having is your being. It is this absolute beauty itself, which is the form that gives being to every form of beauty. O immeasurably lovely Face, your beauty is such that all things to which are granted to behold it are not sufficient to admire it.

—St. Nicholas of Cusa, *On the Vision of God*

It is good that one should wait quietly for the salvation of the Lord.

—Lamentations 3:26

Dietrich Bonhoeffer begins his book *Christ the Center* by saying, "Teaching about Christ begins in silence."[1] What do you think he meant? Why do you think that is? Take a moment to think about it. (Yes, now. Like, right now.) Pause. Breathe. Be silent.

If you're like me, you'll keep reading and forgo the forced exercise. But what does it say about us when we're so reluctant to pause?

1. Bonhoeffer, *Christ the Center*, 27. The idea is not original with Bonhoeffer. He quotes Cyril of Alexandria: "In silence I worship the unutterable."

THE GROWTH OF PRODUCTIVITY AND THE FALL OF STILLNESS

I have a productivity problem. No, I don't have trouble producing. I love getting things done and checking off boxes. I have a problem with finding my worth in what I accomplish. In the truth category, I can read my Bible and check off my daily devotional time. In the goodness category, I can focus on vices and the habits that cultivate virtue. But prayer seems useless because it is so unmeasurable. Experience with the divine can't be manufactured. I rarely leave a prayer time thinking I've done anything at all. It seems like I spent time in my own mind saying things to a God I believe in who may not hear me or care about what I have to say. I can't check anything off. The prayer time doesn't seem to accomplish anything.

In a novel by Wendell Berry called *Jayber Crow*, there's a character named Troy. He's pursuing a love interest and is portrayed as a bit of an antagonist. He eventually marries her, but Berry contrasts Troy with his eventual father-in-law, Athey. Here's what Berry writes: "Athey said, 'Wherever I look, I want to see more than I need.' Troy said, in effect, 'Whatever I see, I want.'"[2] These are two fundamentally different ways of seeing the world, and the latter comes with disastrous effects. The first one cultivates care, margin, and love; the second produces exploitation, efficiency, and apathy.

But doesn't Troy have the modern mindset? Sure, we may not want more land, but we want more stuff. Or in my case, I want more time, more moments to be productive in.

There may be nothing more valuable and more needed in Christian spirituality today than to slow down, to stop trying to do something, and to attend. I'm guessing that if you humored me in the above exercise of silencing yourself, you found that taking a breath, closing your eyes, and sitting still for a moment felt refreshing. It does for me. In my world, I go, go, go, do, do, do, and I need moments when I stop chasing life. As T. S. Eliot eloquently says in his poem "Burnt Norton," I'm regularly "distracted from distraction by distraction."[3]

All theology starts in silence, because before we say anything about God or speculate about God, we need to be reminded that all knowl-

2. Berry, *Jayber Crow*, 182.
3. Eliot, *Four Quartets*, 13.

edge of God comes to us by grace rather than by our own effort or our own pontificating about what we think God is like. Theology starts in silence because silence is where we meet God.[4]

This gift of silence comes to us from the mystical or contemplative tradition. Fred Bahnson has written a memoir about food, land, and spirituality. He spent time at a monastery in South Carolina where he asked his spiritual director about going deeper in prayer. Father Kevin answered, "Limit the input. . . . God pursues *us*. The challenge is to slow down enough to recognize it."[5] I can relate. In my early prayer life, I followed the ACTS plan: Adoration, Confession, Thanksgiving, Supplication. These were the parts of prayer that were necessary for connecting with God. First, I adored God. I said things that are true about him. Sometimes I'd discover a new term, like "omniscient." "God, you are omniscient," I would pray. But I was limited to my concepts. Then, I would confess. Often the sins were the same as last time: the generic, run-of-the-mill things. Maybe I had gotten extra mad that week, so anger would be especially confessed. Then I would thank God. I was confused with this one. It seemed a lot like adoration. So, I would thank God for the same things I adored about him. Then I would make supplications, which meant asking for things.

As I grew older, I ended up with less to say. Words failed me. I thought maybe that was a bad thing, as if I were supposed to have an influx of spiritual language or insights to say to God. I needed to say true things about God. I ought to express my encounter with God, even to remind myself. To be fair, prayer needs theological insight, or

4. There's a whole tradition of theology that emphasizes the silence and unknowability of God. It's called the apophatic tradition, and it highlights the nonconceptual knowledge of God. As a commentary on the Orthodox theologian Vladimir Lossky, Rowan Williams writes, "The source and end of apophatic theology for Lossky is, therefore, a fully conscious (though non-intellectual) relationship of personal confrontation between man and God in love" (*Wrestling with Angels*, 13). Apophatic theology knows that our most eloquent and accurate words still fail to display the full beauty and being of God. God surpasses anything we might say about him. Even if we say God is love, which is thoroughly scriptural, our own idea of love is incompatible with the fullness of God's love. So, in essence, we limit God to our own understanding rather than allow God to be mysterious and incomprehensible. There's a further distinction that says we can speak about God with reference to the way he reveals himself in his energies or attributes (cataphatic theology). But God in his nature or essence will always be inaccessible (apophatic theology).

5. Bahnson, *Soil and Sacrament*, 17.

else it would be vacuous and meaningless. Yet when explanations and understandings and descriptions ran out, I sat in the divine presence and wanted to experience God. My words were inadequate. They always were. In silence, Thomas Merton reminds us, God ceases to be an object and becomes an experience.[6]

The beautiful life, according to a mystic or contemplative, is not one of technique. I can't offer you four steps to become a mystic. We live in a technological age in which growth can be condensed into steps. The temptation for me is to view the contemplative life as some sort of achievement or project. *If I devote thirty minutes a day to quiet prayer, in six months I will have increased my spirituality by 25 percent*, I think. But as Thomas Merton explains in his book on contemplation, "The worst disadvantage of contemplation is that it sounds like 'something,' an objective quality, a spiritual commodity that one can procure, something that is good to have; something which, when possessed, liberates one from problems and from unhappiness."[7] Contemplation is not a goal that one reaches. It is not a manufactured project. Christianity is an encounter with a person, not an idea.

As such, the beauty tradition requires learning to listen more than it requires knowing what to say. Perhaps I can call the first step to prayer a "sanctified shutting up." In its essence the beauty tradition is about the practices of living more humanly. Rowan Williams recommends a slow life of listening as "living with less frantic acquisitiveness, living with space for stillness, living in the expectation of learning, and most of all, living with an awareness that there is a solid and durable *joy* to be discovered in the disciplines of self-forgetfulness that is quite different from the gratification of this or that impulse of the moment."[8] A beautiful life is in beholding the Beautiful One.

GOD AS BEAUTY

Describing God as beautiful may be new for you. It was for me when I first heard it done. I could imagine God as true. He could be known

6. Merton, *No Man Is an Island*, 268.
7. Merton, *New Seeds of Contemplation*, x.
8. Williams, *Holy Living*, 101–2.

by a philosopher-theologian. I could imagine God as good. He could be studied by a practical or moral theologian. But beautiful? That seemed subjective, too personal. I would need to become a lover or mystic for that. Yet God is not just a being we know or react to; as the Beautiful One, he also compels us and draws us in.

Rather than define beauty according to what it *is*, I think it's more helpful to define beauty according to what it *does*. Beauty demands attention. Beauty draws something out of us. Thomas Aquinas defines it as that which pleases upon being seen.[9] Beauty stops us in our tracks and slows us down. If we think about beauty less didactically and more experientially, we'll see beauty is a fairly good description of God. God, like a work of art, slows us, compels us, pleases us, draws something out of us.

And if God is beauty, then being unbiased or disinterested about the Beautiful One is impossible. It would be like trying to explain my wife cooly and rationally. I suppose I could. I could tell you facts about her. She has brown hair and brown eyes. She likes organization and tidiness. She's servant-hearted. Yet as true as all those facts are, they don't capture who my wife is. They don't explain her. Someone who wanted to see what makes her lovely would have to know her, spend time with her. It's similar with God. We should not be cold and analytical about God. We are experiencing a beauty, a love, that we cannot comprehend.

I said in the introduction to this book that the transcendentals are called such since they point to the Transcendent One, in whose image we are made. God, then, is the epitome of beauty. He displays his beautiful essence in his first creative act. Evoking the poem of creation in Genesis 1, Makoto Fujimura has written, "God the Artist communicates to us first, before God the lecturer."[10] God starts the Bible with a divine poem. In response to the creation of woman, man's response is not a doctrine but a song: "Bone of my bones and flesh of my flesh . . ." (Gen. 2:23). When Christ comes in the incarnation, Mary responds not with an email but with an ode.[11] Quoting Saint John Chrysostom, Thomas Merton writes, "The angels do not

9. Aquinas, *Summa Theologica* I-II, 27.1.
10. Fujimura, *Art and Faith*, 7.
11. Gioia, "Christianity and Poetry."

'discuss the divine essence' . . . , but they 'sing triumphal and mystic odes.'"[12] The whole of Christian witness is one in which people see beauty and respond as humans do to any beauty: with awe, wonder, contemplation, song. We don't respond to a beautiful song or poem or artwork by explaining what it means. We encounter it, and we are changed by it in a way that's difficult to express. Beauty transforms theology from articulation to contemplation. This is the theological method—not commenting dryly on a divine being but extolling, with the beauty due to his name, the praises of the One who reigns in beauty. Saint Ephrem the Syrian was an early monastic who wrote his theology primarily in poetry rather than prose because poetry opens people up to wonder and awe that invites contemplation. Theology is not a mere intellectual exercise in which one speculates about philosophical concepts. It is communion with the living God.

If God is the paradigm of beauty, then Christ's crucifixion reenvisions what we consider beautiful, because the cross most clearly reveals God's character. It's where his love, his essence, is most evident. The Swiss theologian Hans Urs von Balthasar connects sacrificial love to beauty. His work assists the reader in seeing what exactly is beautiful and thus compelling. The vision von Balthasar unfolds is a beauty of the cruciform. If beauty is a transcendental founded in God, then the quintessential form of beauty is seen on the cross. The cross is the paradigm of beauty, as it is where love is most clearly seen. Glory is the experience of beauty, and the most glorious event in the history of the world, so argues von Balthasar, is the crucifixion of Christ for sinners. Beauty is seen in the gruesome reality of the cross.[13] It's this beauty that leads to goodness and truth. At the foot of a suffering Savior, the onlooker sees the pinnacle of goodness and the pathway to truth. Beauty is not prettiness but a revelation

12. Merton, *Course in Christian Mysticism*, 47.
13. "Insofar as the veil over the face of Christ's mystery is drawn aside, and insofar as the economy of grace allows, Christian contemplation can marvel, in the self-emptying of divine love, at the exceeding wisdom, truth and beauty inherent there. But it is only in this self-emptying that they can be contemplated, for it is the source whence the glory contemplated by the angels and the saints radiated into eternal life. . . . The humiliation of the servant only makes the concealed glory shine more resplendently, and the descent into the ordinary and commonplace brings out the uniqueness of him who so abased himself" (von Balthasar, *Explorations in Theology*, 1:133–34).

of the truest reality and love in the world. Matthias Grünewald's *Is-enheim Altarpiece*—a work of art depicting Christ a little off-center, stretched out in inhumane ways with a greenish, ghoulish tint to his skin—displays divine love more than would a serene setting without anguish or pain. It's beautiful and compelling. It draws us in. It's awe-inspiring. It's where we see love.

The church needs a recovery of its mission of portraying the beautiful in an ugly world. Art and poetry have been a spiritual discipline for me because the theology I grew up with deadened me to wonder and contemplation. I wanted explanations, not wonder. Art and poetry slow down my pragmatic and consumeristic ways. Sitting with a story reduces my production. A poem cannot be condensed into a punch line. Visual art draws me in and takes me outside of myself to focus on another. Often, we don't allow the Bible to penetrate us because we're after quick and pat answers. We ask what difference it makes rather than allowing it to make a difference in our imagination. Beauty may be uncomfortable to theological minds because it lacks clear explanations, tight rationale. It's open to the mysterious and invites multiple interpretations. As Robin Jensen observes, "If we reflect upon something of beauty long enough, we should begin to be like it. If we study an image of horror or suffering, we will be moved to rage or pity. If these are only passing responses, we will not be truly changed. But if we are changed at all, if the images take root in us, we will act differently in the world."[14] Beauty has the power to change us if we attend to it.

Attending is the challenge. Amid the busyness of life, slowing down to contemplate, to attend to something we may not understand right away, is hard work. It requires the death of our ego; it requires us to get out of the way, to see from another angle. Contemplation requires a pure desire, an integrated desire, to see God. So often, our passions and desires disintegrate us and pull us in a thousand directions. Beauty awakens us to wonder, and it takes us further into beauty itself. C. S. Lewis writes, "We do not want merely to *see* beauty, though, God knows, even that is bounty enough. We want something else which can hardly be put into words—to be united with the beauty we see, to pass into it, to receive it into ourselves, to bathe

14. Jensen, *Substance of Things Seen*, 21.

in it, to become part of it."[15] Being absorbed into beauty requires a slowness, a death of the desire to produce and acquire. Seeing portrayals of beauty by artists or in the material world can prime us to see the epitome of beauty, the Transcendent One. Throughout the entire scriptural narrative, we are invited to gaze upon God's beauty. He wants us to encounter him in love and, seeing him, to become absorbed in him.

THE STORY OF BEAUTY IN THE BIBLE

In the beginning, God created men and women after his likeness and in his image (Gen. 1:26–27). Irenaeus describes glory this way: "For the glory of God is a living man; and the life of man consists of beholding God."[16] The goal of our life has always been to be intimate with God—to walk with him in the garden (3:8), to see him—and through this intimacy to become more and more like him.

When the serpent enters the garden scene, he causes Adam and Eve to doubt the truth and goodness of God. But there's also another temptation hidden behind the devil's lies. Satan promises that when they eat the fruit, they will be like God (Gen. 3:5). But weren't they already made in the image of God? What was the serpent promising— becoming Godlike apart from the presence of God? Whatever the case may be, the result of such a desire is not greater intimacy but alienation. They were created for intimacy with God, but in a moment, that closeness with God is robbed from them. A chasm erupts. Rather than know God face to face, Adam and Eve hide in fear. God asks a question: "Where are you?" (3:9). God still wants intimacy while they cower in shame, hiding from the One who loved them into life.

The rest of human history follows this pattern: God desires intimacy with his creation, and his creation perpetually hides from him in sin. At times in the story of Israel, different people get close. They desire to see God, but sin is still a major obstacle. We see this pattern in Moses's leadership in Egypt and at Sinai.[17]

---

15. Lewis, *Made for Heaven*, 85–86.
16. Irenaeus, *Against Heresies* 4.20.7 (Keble, 444).
17. For a fuller treatment of Moses in Exodus, see Gregory of Nyssa, *Life of Moses*.

In Exodus 3, Moses sees a burning bush that is not being consumed and discovers it is the divine presence. God invites Moses into participation with him. He will use Moses to lead Israel out of Egypt. Then, after Moses receives the Ten Commandments (Exod. 20), the text reports, "The people stood far off, while Moses drew near to the thick darkness where God was" (v. 21). Here the theophany, or vision of God, is depicted as beyond knowledge or human comprehension—as taking place through a cloud of thick darkness. From a bush to a cloud.

God gives the details for building the tabernacle, which will replace the pillar of cloud and fire as the special place of his presence with his people (Exod. 26–27). While these details are being relayed to Moses, the people build a false god (32:1–6). Again, they choose intimacy with a false god, with a created image, rather than the true Creator God. God could, and perhaps should, destroy the people he recently rescued. Yet he relents. He will work with and in Israel. In the third revelation, God reveals himself again to Moses. Moses wants to see God's face and to know his name. This time, God reveals his back as Moses is sheltered in the cleft of a rock (33:18–23). From bush to cloud to the back of God. Gregory of Nyssa comments, "And although lifted up through such lofty experiences, [Moses] is still unsatisfied in his desire for more. He still thirsts for that with which he constantly filled himself to capacity, and he asks to attain as if he had never partaken, beseeching God to appear to him, not according to his capacity to partake, but according to God's true being."[18] Moses still has more paths to travel and more to know. The knowledge of God cannot be exhausted, even if Moses has experienced more in Exodus 33 than he did in Exodus 3.

In the fullness of time the final revelation of God comes in the person of his Son. No longer is God pictured in the priesthood or sacrificial system. God has spoken in various ways in different times through different means (see Heb. 1:1), but Jesus comes as the "radiance of the glory of God and the exact imprint of his nature" (1:3) and "the image of the invisible God" (Col. 1:15). Anyone who looks on Christ has seen the Father (John 14:8–11). God finally comes to dwell among

18. Gregory of Nyssa, *Life of Moses*, 114.

us, and we gaze upon his glory, "full of grace and truth" (John 1:14). While death, sin, and nature separate us from God, Christ comes to reconcile us in reverse order. Vladimir Lossky references Nicholas Cabasilas, "a Byzantine theologian from the fourteenth century, who said on this subject, 'The Lord allowed men, separated from God by the triple barrier of nature, sin and death, to be fully possessed of Him and to be directly united to Him by the fact he has set aside each barrier in turn: that of nature by his incarnation, of sin by His death, and of death by His resurrection.'"[19] Christ tears down the dividing wall so that we can commune with God in himself.

Different saints in history have described seeing God in different ways but to the same effect. The term they developed is *theosis*, or "deification," and it is meant to convey that, in Christ, our goal is to become gods. Saint Peter says we are to become "partakers of the divine nature" (2 Pet. 1:4). Saint Irenaeus puts it this way: "The Word of God, our Lord Jesus Christ . . . did, through His transcendent love, become what we are, that He might bring us to be even what He is Himself."[20] Saint Athanasius more succinctly wrote, "He was incarnate that we might be made gods."[21] God comes down to make himself known in human terms (most notably in the incarnation) so that we may ascend to God.[22] These early church fathers weren't merely arguing that Jesus came to make us holy. They were arguing that he came to make us gods. Bold claims!

In Christ we become what we behold. Charles Taylor translates a passage from Saint Augustine as "Everyone becomes like what he loves. Dost thou love the earth? Thou shalt be earth. Dost thou love God? Then I say, thou shalt be God."[23] Looking at the God we love,

---

19. Lossky, *Mystical Theology of the Eastern Church*, 136.

20. Irenaeus, *Against Heresies* 6.11 (Keble, 449).

21. Athanasius, *On the Incarnation* 54.3 (Behr, 107).

22. The Orthodox tradition makes a distinction between the essence and energies of God. By becoming absorbed in the energies, we become God, though we never partake or share in God's essence. His energies are his grace. We know God through his energies but have no access to his essence. On this, Michael Horton notes, "So there is deification without pantheism, union without fusion" (Horton, *Christian Faith*, 691).

23. Taylor, *Sources of the Self*, 128. There's another quote credited to Saint Bernard of Clairvaux, but I haven't found documentation for it. Along Augustinian lines, it says, "What we love we shall grow to resemble."

"we all, with unveiled face, beholding the glory of the Lord, are being transformed into the same image from one degree of glory to another. For this comes from the Lord who is the Spirit" (2 Cor. 3:18). Since Christ has torn down the barrier that separated us from God, we are able to participate in the life of God in Jesus Christ. We are united to him and are being transformed by him.

This transformation is beyond knowledge or activity. We return to the core of our being, which is a truer image bearer of God, as we see the true image of God. Before we are a slave to sin or unique personality or success story or failure, we are divine creations. Even if that inner reality is twisted by our choices or shrouded by distraction, we are sacred beings living before our Maker. We make ever-increasing progress in this life with God, but like Moses, we are never satisfied in the desire to see him. There's always more to see and experience.

THE LORD'S SUPPER AS SEEING GOD

We live in a world full of noise and distraction. Sometimes our theological conversation can be noisy too. In the prayer journey I described earlier in the chapter, I arrived at a place where I was tired of talking. I wanted to sit in God's presence. When words ran out, I wanted to taste and see. I desired encounters with God and wanted to participate with God rather than conjecture about him.

I desired intimacy. The good news of the gospel is that God desires divine-human intimacy more than I do. Christ made himself available to humanity—to the worst of sinners! To sinners like me and like you. The desire of God to be with his creation was fulfilled at the steepest of costs in the death of his Son.

Now God invites us into greater intimacy with himself in the form of bread and wine. Christ, in a real but mysterious way, is present to us in the Eucharist. We consume the mystery of Jesus and become consumed by him. We eat, and God becomes part of us. We are nourished by the bread that was consumed for us. God invites us to enter this great mystery through tasting. In the Lord's Supper, we contemplate Christ. With eyes of faith, we see him in the Eucharist.

In the schema of Saint Thomas Aquinas, the sacraments are inherently tied to what they are used for, which, he argues, is making human beings holy.[24] The Eucharist is a means to the beatific vision, seeing God. The bread and wine aren't turned in on themselves but are turned upward to become a divine encounter.[25] John McDermott describes the sacramental understanding as the realization that the "material world serves as a communicator of God to man and as a means of enabling him to attain the beautifying possession of God in His kingdom."[26] In a mysterious manner we take God within us. And Christ works on transforming us from the inside out.

CONCLUSION

Growing up, I loved Kobe Bryant. I joined his fan club, collected his trading cards, got his autograph, and went to see him play. I loved him, so I tried to resemble him. I worked on his iconic step-back fadeaway over and over. With the clock running out (in my imaginative mind), I attempted the iconic shot: *Three!* I dribbled around the defender. *Two!* I picked up the dribble. *One!* I made a jab step, did a fade, and shot—*Kobe!* Sometimes it went in. But Kobe was clutch. He made it all the time, I thought. I loved Kobe, so I tried to resemble him, even though I was a short, stocky white guy.

This is the way love works. We resemble what we love, even if the creature-Creator distinction is vast, even if sin plagues us. I saw Kobe only on a screen or from a distance in an arena. God invites us into his very life. He comes close to us in Christ. God wants us to spend time with him, to see him in his beauty, to contemplate him, to be transformed.

Often, I can view my life with a selfish lens. I can be so focused on Bible studies or ascetic practices or writing or reading theology that I neglect the goal. I think it's all about me—about me becoming a certain type of person or having a skill set or knowledge base. But beauty takes me out of myself. It focuses me on a greater goal: union with God.

24. Thomas Aquinas, *Summa Theologica* III.lx.2c and ad 1.
25. Boersma, "Sacramental Journey to the Beatific Vision," 1021.
26. McDermott, *Love and Understanding*, 299.

✳ 8 ✳

The ROAD to TRANSFORMATION and UNION

ATTENTION, CONTEMPLATION, AND DETACHMENT

To pray is to pay attention or, shall we say, to "listen" to someone or something other than oneself. Whenever a man so concentrates his attention—be it on a landscape, or a poem or a geometrical problem or an idol or the True God—that he completely forgets his own ego and desires in listening to what the other has to say to him, he is praying.

—W. H. Auden, "Work, Carnival, Prayer"

Nothing is more essential to prayer than attentiveness.
—Evagrius of Pontus, *On Prayer*

In the film *Lady Bird*, directed by Greta Gerwig, the main character gives herself the name Lady Bird after rejecting her given name,
Christine.[1] Throughout the movie she rails against traditional limits
and wants to escape the deadbeat town of Sacramento to go to the
East Coast ("where good schools are"). Toward the end of the movie,
she's meeting with a nun over a disciplinary matter at her Catholic
high school. She put a "just married" sign on a car that two of the
nuns drive. While meeting, the nun brings up her college essay and
remarks, "You clearly love Sacramento."

Shocked, Lady Bird looks up. "I do?"

The nun continues, "You write about Sacramento so affection-
ately and with such care."

Lady Bird responds, "I was just describing it."

"Well, it comes across as love."

"Sure, I guess I pay attention."

The nun ends the scene: "Don't you think maybe they're the same
thing? Love? Attention?"

In the previous chapter we saw that we become what we behold,
and I want us to see at the beginning of this chapter that we pay attention to what we love. Attention starts not in effort but in interest,
desire, wanting to know more. Luke Bell argues along the same lines
when he insists, "Giving whole attention to Him, whom to know
is to love, is to live. This is why recovering a contemplative spirit
matters."[2] Contemplation, attention, is the way we love God. It's
the way to the good life.

The contemplative life starts in prayer or in the church, but if your
prayer and attention are limited to those fixed hours or moments,
then the contemplative spirit is lost. Prayer is meant to extend beyond
the set times and expand out into the world as it is—into the fields
and parishes and workplaces and art galleries. The material world
reveals the spiritual. Creation reveals the Creator. The goal of our
times of contemplation is that the practice would turn into our life.
This vision is the dynamic at play in the writings of Brother Lawrence,
a French mystic of the seventeenth century. He sees everything turn

1. I use this example in an article on education and attention. See Sosler, "Attentional Arts and Beholding Beauty."
2. Bell, *Meaning of Blue*, 84.

to prayer. In his case, doing dishes becomes close to contemplative ecstasy. God can be found in all mundane work—from doing the dishes to changing a diaper, from studying for a test to completing spreadsheets. Everything can be done with contemplative awareness in the presence of God.

This way of life is sacramental, like the Lord's Supper. All things reveal God if we have eyes to see. Hans Boersma suggests that "in as much as the natural world around is a self-manifestation of God, he uses every one of the physical senses to draw us into his presence."[3] All the set times of contemplative prayer are meaningless if they don't affect our ability to see the presence of God in the world. Stop and consider: holiness is all around us. How often are we aware of it?

Since the world is sacramental, it is worth seeing. The astonishing thing about God as the Beautiful One is that he creates all things with hints of beauty. Therefore, even if we live too fast to see it, the world is worth noticing. Chef and author Gregory Thompson, in his quarterly newsletter in *Comment* magazine, reflects on living with and in nature. He writes, "Contemplation may be understood as a form of confrontation—a struggle to see in the midst of blindness and to love in the midst of neglect. Contemplation is not, despite popular sentiment, a movement away from the world, but a movement toward it with a deepened commitment to love."[4] God is at work in the materiality of world, loving it into existence. We're invited to pay attention. Norman Wirzba expands this sentiment in what he calls an "agrarian mysticism" that says "God is always with and within creatures as their creating, animating, nurturing, and sustaining Source. There is no such thing as a world without God."[5] That is, God is to be found not up and away but down and around. He is nearer us than our inward selves are. He is mysteriously present in the material world.

3. Boersma, *Seeing God*, 219. On the sacramental nature of the world, Boersma writes, "Christian contemplation, therefore, is a sacramental way of seeing: It means we approach creation and the Scriptures as filled with the presence of Christ" (*Seeing God*, 232).

4. Thompson, "To Inhabit the Earth."

5. Wirzba, *Agrarian Spirit*, 115.

If we attend to the world this way, with the understanding that God is immanent within it, the way we treat the world will change. This contemplative vision will address the fragmentation of our lives and our alienation from others. We will begin to see the spiritual oneness of all things—not in a way that flattens the creature-Creator distinction but in a way that enriches the material and relational world. The way we treat the world is the way we treat each other, and it goes the other way around too: the way we treat each other is the way we treat the world.

Here's the paradox of attention: in prayer, as we give our attention to God, we come to realize that, rather than our gaze resting upon God, God's gaze rests upon us. John of the Cross says, "Preserve a loving attentiveness to God with no desire to feel or understand any particular thing concerning God."[6] After all, the emotions one has in prayer are not the point. The essential movement of prayer is cultivating a return to the present moment. We return again and again to the God who gazes upon us and who first desires intimacy with us.

CONTEMPLATION

Contemplation is very far from being just one kind of thing that Christians do: it is the key to prayer, liturgy, art and ethics, the key to the essence of a renewed humanity that is capable of seeing the world and other subjects in the world with freedom—freedom from self-oriented, acquisitive habits and the distorted understanding that comes from these. To put it boldly, contemplation is the only ultimate answer to the unreal and insane world that our financial systems and our advertising culture and our chaotic and unexamined emotions encourage us to inhabit. To learn contemplative practice is to learn to live truthfully and honestly and lovingly.

—Rowan Williams, *Holy Living*

I have a confession: I am a beginner in contemplative practice. You may have picked that up from how I described my desire for productivity. So often, I'm distracted by my own internal monologue or the

6. John of the Cross, "Maxim on Love, 88," 674.

task at hand that I don't notice God, who wants to reveal himself in every moment of the day. I'm like a dog who sees a squirrel— constantly shifting attention to thoughts that flow into my mind with ease. If you ever take time to attend, you'll notice the chattiness of your internal monologue too. Just this morning, as I was spending time in silence, I was also meta-reflecting on my reflection the entire time. I'm trying to attend to the moment, but my internal chatter is reflecting on what I'm doing, wondering if this is working, wondering why I'm thinking about my thinking, unable to do the sanctified shutting up that's necessary. There's internal monologue about internal monologue, and then there's more internal monologue trying to control that internal monologue. It can be exhausting. It's hard for me to be still and silent.

I'm a beginner, trying to make progress. In the contemplative tradition, we're all amateurs. It's not something we master. Here are a few things I've learned that have helped me attend along the way.

Contemplation is not special knowledge for elites. All the initiative lies in the loving-kindness of God, who wants to reveal himself to us. The contemplative practice attempts to remove obstacles that stand in the way of communion and encounter. Therefore, this intimate, even experiential, knowledge of God, "far from being something essentially extraordinary, like visions, revelations, or the stigmata, *is in the normal way of sanctity.*"[7] Demanding more than a vision of God or desiring some other imaginative experience is akin to asking for a second incarnation. God has been known through Christ. Therefore, listen to him—which is another way of saying, "Pay attention to him."[8] Contemplation is the way we cultivate attention.

One of the most helpful ways to start is to have a phrase or word to return to. Historically, the Jesus Prayer has been used: "Lord, Jesus Christ, Son of the living God, have mercy on me, a sinner" (cf. Luke 18:13). Different traditions include different words ("God," "love,"

---

7. Garrigou-Lagrange, *Three Ages of the Interior Life*, 1:103–5.

8. The language of "paying attention," which uses monetary terms, is interesting. It's almost as if we owe certain things attention and we pay for it. Contemplation may cost us something.

"maranatha"). Whichever word or sentence you choose, it has the same purpose: slowing the mind and reigning in straying thoughts in order to achieve focus over distraction.[9] Saying the word or sentence in rhythm with our breathing can also bring a somatic unity in which our body and our thoughts are united to bring attention. In contemplation the goal is to return to the love of God that is present in each moment. It's an astonishing reality, really: God wants to reveal his love to us, and we're so distracted and busy we hardly notice it. As Thomas Keating suggests, "All spiritual exercises are designed to reduce the monumental illusion that God is absent."[10] Repeating a word or sentence can help us return in order to catch a glimpse of God's present love for us in a given moment.

Repeating a word or sentence can also be a means by which the Spirit helps us in our weakness to gain understanding. For example, the Jesus Prayer says the truth of who Christ is and who we are. These truths, repeated, draw us deeper into the mystery of the truth of Christ and our sinful state. Commenting on Evagrius, who defined prayer as habitual intimacy, Thomas Merton writes, "This disposes us to accept the idea that prayer is immediate intuitive contact with God, a habitual commerce with God, not a conversation in words or thoughts."[11] Again, the contemplative goal in prayer is not personal expression. There's a place for that. But in contemplation we seek the face of God in an encounter. We strive to be content in his presence.

To prepare, expect mental distractions and wandering thoughts. Internal dialogue is inevitable, and all the more so as you start off. The important thing is how you meet distraction. As the contemplative writer Martin Laird suggests, "How we meet distraction (not whether or not we experience distractions—this is a given) is what heals and transforms as we move deeper."[12] Laird offers three questions to ponder as we go through distractions.[13]

9. As Thomas Keating has suggested, "the goal of contemplative prayer is not so much the emptiness of thoughts or conversation as the emptiness of self" (Keating, *Intimacy with God*, 125).

10. Keating, *Intimacy with God*, 73.

11. Merton, *Course in Christian Mysticism*, 63.

12. Laird, *Into the Silent Land*, 76.

13. Laird, *Into the Silent Land*, 77, 80, 89.

I. "ARE YOU YOUR THOUGHTS AND FEELINGS?"

As you begin a contemplative practice, attending to God, there will be a roommate who plays music or a neighbor who cuts the grass or a child who walks in. In short, you will meet frustration or anger, because the setting is not ideal. In those moments, you will again face the challenge of inner commentary. "That jerk roommate!" "That inconsiderate neighbor!" "These meddling kids!" But the goal is to meet all these external situations in stillness. You are not your feelings of annoyance. You are not your reaction. You may feel bound by these reactions, but they are not the self. The goal of contemplation is to meet chaos with peace, to respond to distractions with stillness rather than commentary.

When you start out, these distracting thoughts may be prevalent. Moreover, in day-to-day life we often ignore deep feelings of abandonment or issues of self-worth, and when we finally are still, these negative feelings can rise like a tide in our souls. Things long past and seemingly forgotten can storm in and overwhelm us. In silence we learn to deal with them. Rather than justifying these thoughts away, we meet negative feelings with a self-knowledge. We notice them. We ask questions. We let them pass. We are not the sum total of our thoughts and feelings.

2. "WHAT DO THOUGHTS AND FEELINGS APPEAR IN?"

As we move from *being* our thoughts and feelings to *noticing* our thoughts and feelings, we change from a victim to a witness. We have agency with our thoughts and feelings. In verbiage from the Psalms, we ask our own soul, "Why are you cast down, O my soul, and why are you in turmoil within me?" (Pss. 42:5, 11; 43:5). We have the ability to speak back to our feelings. *Why are you upset, soul? Who makes you this way? Why? When? How? To what effect?*

By becoming aware of the thoughts that bring misery, we can observe them, let them pass like a river running through our mind—here one moment, gone the next—and return to the loving awareness of God. We are not our feelings, even if they seem like they bind and enslave us. We give commentary to our feelings, but we can meet the feeling before the commentary. Watch it come. Watch it go. As

Laird comments, "Affliction feeds off the noise of the commenting, chattering mind."[14] So often, I judge myself in prayer while in prayer. *Am I doing this right? Will this be fruitful?* I remember a certain time of "fruitful" prayer, and I want to recreate it. But that's more chatter and distraction. Meet all these straying thoughts with a silent, steady gaze.

In the contemplative tradition the self is often compared to a mountain. The weather is the noise of the world, even the noise of our own thoughts and changing emotions. When the noise of weather comes, the contemplative tradition invites us to realize that we need not be swayed by all the noise. So often, we feel lost in the weather, as if the weather is who we are. When it's cold, we're cold. When anger comes, we're angry. But contemplation helps us realize that we are not our emotions or circumstances. All that noise is going on around us, but it is not the self. We can be as unmoved as a mountain. As Rowan Williams writes, "Learning discernment is first learning how to identify and bring to stillness the urge to reduce the world to the terms of my desires; in other words, it is to do with learning to observe and question whatever forms of controlling power I possess."[15] We can notice feelings or circumstances as we notice the weather. We can't control it, but we can see it; and the weather need not erode us. Mountains don't change with the weather.

3. "WHAT IS THE NATURE OF THESE THOUGHTS AND FEELINGS, AND WHO IS AWARE OF THEM?"

The last question Laird asks is one that requires deeper consideration. Laird mentions the author of *The Cloud of Unknowing*, who says that whenever you are plagued by distractions, "try to look over their shoulders, as it were, searching for something else—and that something is God, enclosed in the cloud of unknowing."[16] One of the beautiful things I've experienced in contemplation is the melting away of my hard heart. It's hard to be self-righteous and judge others when we can look beyond anger and frustration to see God.

14. Laird, *Into the Silent Land*, 106.
15. Williams, *Looking East in Winter*, 192.
16. *The Cloud of Unknowing*, 55.

Sometimes, when not in contemplation, I focus on a frustrating person or situation but never move beyond the feeling. Contemplation gives me the opportunity to do just that: to look beyond the frustration. Contemplation takes desolation and turns it into freedom. It allows us to enter a vast spaciousness that connects all things and holds them together, a spaciousness where there is a deep belonging at the center of existence that invites us into a transformation that gives us empathy for ourselves and others.

Fred Bahnson describes having such an experience on a journalistic assignment to Mali with *Harper's Magazine*. After declining to go to a meeting in a dangerous part of Gao with a monk named Colombo, he reflected on his childhood, which included a three-year stint of living away from his parents as they pursued a vocation as medical missionaries. He says that this distance between family and home was miserable. He cried himself to sleep and learned never to complain, as both he and his parents were "doing it for the Lord." However, this rationale didn't comfort the heart of the ten-year-old child. He harbored resentment and pain from those early years, and they came to surface these many years later in the same continent where he suffered as a child. But here's how he reflected on his pain:

> Those years injured my soul, but they'd also given me a gift. Through my childhood experience of solitary prayer and my adult discovery of monastic spirituality, I had found a path that led to a wider expanse. The monastic project showed me how to turn loneliness into solitude. The early monks' great discovery was that we are each a monos: the walls of the self are the burden of every human. They also discovered that the vulnerability of solitary prayer makes those walls more porous, leading us out of ourselves and into communion with our neighbors. Solitude begets solidarity.[17]

"Solitude begets solidarity"—that's a great phrase. He didn't retreat into himself to find himself. The monastic tradition invites us to be still and to notice that the walls of selfhood are rather porous. We grow closer to other people as we grow closer to God. The walls

17. Bahnson, "Guardians of Memory."

that separate us from others, the walls on which we stand in judgment over others, begin to crumble. This oneness does not erase the distinctiveness of individual creatures, but it is a recognition that the sustenance and source of all things comes in and through God. Alone, Bahnson became aware of the source of the real and of the life that he shared with all created beings.

I can't imagine sending my kids away for three years, even for a supposedly noble purpose like serving God. Bahnson's parents bear some responsibility for the unintentional hurt they may have caused. But he doesn't let their decision drive him to hate them or consider himself a victim of their choices. He notices the pain, but he does not dwell there. Through contemplative prayer he becomes the mountain that the weather passes around. Or rather, he knows that his "life is hidden with Christ in God" (Col. 3:3) and that God is the mountain of refuge and strength. In so doing he becomes a more empathetic person as he sees the seeds of God slowly bearing fruit, even in rocky soil.

HOLY DETACHMENT

> One of the paradoxes of the mystical life is this: that *a man cannot enter into the deepest center of himself and pass through that center into God, unless he is able to pass entirely out of himself and empty himself and give himself to other people in the purity of a selfless love.*
>
> —Thomas Merton, *New Seeds of Contemplation*

The contemplative life starts in desire. We desire to know and see and encounter Christ. We want to see his face. We love him. Yet desire, unavoidable though it may be for humans, is dangerous and often gets people into trouble. Desire is the root of many horrible sins and tragedies in our world. So, then, what are we to do with our passions, and how do they fit in with faithful contemplation? It's a question I've thought about a lot because I live with and in passion. Ever since I was young, my passions seemed uncontrollable—as much a part of me as the color of my hair or the pigment of my skin. In playing sports, I "wore my heart on my sleeve," as the saying goes. Nobody had to ask how I was feeling; they knew. I was distraught if we lost or ecstatic if we won. That was my authentic self. Later, when my passions overwhelmed me and those around me, I learned to push my passions down and never bring them up again.

In our modern world, passion plays an elusive role. Are my passions my truest self, the most authentic me? Should I express them no matter what and decide that it's not my fault if others don't like them? Or, like Elsa from *Frozen*, should I conceal, don't feel, don't let them know? Or should we let it go?

There's something in Ignatian spirituality called "holy detachment." We are born with passionate desire, yet to experience God we must put to death selfish passion and self-centered desire. In essence, holy detachment invites us to care only about the things that help us love God and love neighbor. In all other things we should be passionless, detached, in some ways indifferent to whole swaths of human existence. Desire isn't to be rejected; it is to be discipled. This discipleship process requires a rejection of the self-directed and reactionary passions. As Rowan Williams puts it, "The holy person is one 'free from passion' because he or she is the person free from having their relations totally dictated by instinct, self-defense—reactivity, as we might say these days."[18] A free person is one who has passions but who is not controlled by those passions in a reactive cycle.

Imagine for a moment what it would be like if you stopped caring what other people thought of you. You may think that would be rude; part of a life of love is caring about people and their feelings. But imagine that you stopped trying to make good impressions, that you could walk away from an encounter and not play over in your mind how you came across. Imagine that you didn't care about what your friends thought of you. What jokes would you not make? What posts would you make (or not make) on social media? Would you care about social media at all? How much do you currently do for others' approval, to fit in? What do you refrain from doing so that your friends will still think you're cool? What would you not post about if you weren't concerned with being on the right side of an issue? What would it be like if you didn't desperately care about what grade you earned? And maybe part of your motivation to earn the

---

18. Williams, *Holy Living*, 119.

grade you're striving for is really about appeasing your parents or teacher. Put all those passions aside.

How would you relate to a spouse or significant other if your passions weren't primary, and you could see her as a gift in her own particularity, and you related to her as God relates to her? Being emptied of your preferences, what would it look like for you to love your children without trying to manipulate or control them, instead caring for them and seeing them as uniquely bearing the image of God in their own giftedness?

What would it look like for your church to live in holy detachment, to love others without interest in their own passions but, instead, for the mutual love of God?

What if we rejected our own passions in order to gain the passions that help us love God and love neighbor? Holy detachment does not mean that I'm passionless for my kids or wife or neighbors. But I lay down the demands my passions make and regard others as God sees them. I lay down my passions and take up the "passion"—in the other sense of the word, the sense of suffering—of Christ, which is the way of the cross.

This may sound like a quasi-Stoic or quasi-Buddhist ethic—the goal of life is one of detaching oneself from the world and from cares. The Buddha himself left his own family in pursuit of a detached life. Even the attachment to family was a hindrance to a holy life. But holy detachment does not veer into the unhelpful notion of placelessness and namelessness. It is not that God loves us without distinction. He loves the essence of us as it relates to his own essence. We share in bearing God's image in unique ways with our unique personalities and makeup. In the same way, in Christ, adopted by God, we are to love others in their own particularity and from our own place. We are free to recognize the interconnectedness of all—that this person shares God with me through our mutual bearing of the divine image. Yet we still maintain a distinction of particularity in how each Christian displays the essence of God in themselves. Christians are like each other in significant ways, yet their own distinctions make them different in more profound ways. Those differences can be causes for consternation or reasons to rejoice. The call to love one another is a call to love people without reference to one's own preference or affinity but rather in a way that reflects the indiscriminate love of God. God has a general love for the whole of humanity, but what makes God even more amazing is that he has a particular love for each one of us.

After all, prayer is not about us. It is about God. When we express all our concerns to God, we call God to attend to us. There are times for that. But our goal is to be detached from our concerns so that we turn from our interests to the goodness and love of God. It's only in prayer that we can start to lose grip on our own passions and become passionate about something beyond the self. As Rabbi Abraham Heschel commends, "The purpose of prayer is not the same as the purpose of speech. The purpose of speech is to inform; the purpose of prayer is to partake."[19] Those who have reached a holy detachment can care about the things that God cares about and can begin to partake of him.

TRANSFORMATION

In a fascinating article about bourbon and spiritual formation, art professor Matthew Milliner tells a story of his visit to Kentucky's bourbon country. This isn't to say that bourbon is helpful to spiritual formation, and in certain contexts and times, it may be detrimental to spiritual formation. But he compares the process by which we are formed with the process by which bourbon is produced, and he uncovers interesting parallels. Through his travels he had a realization: bourbon country is also God's country. In Kentucky, spirits and the spiritual sit side by side. Historic basilicas and convents are located near modern distilleries. The sacred and the secular seem inseparable. Considering these twin realities, Milliner concludes that distilling bourbon requires the same steps as spiritual formation: purgation, illumination, union.[20]

PURGATION

The first step of transformation is purgation. Just as the corn for bourbon is harvested, crushed, and fermented in its own death, so a Christian spirituality requires a type of death. Saint John of

19. Heschel, *Between God and Man*, 202.
20. Milliner, "Becoming Bourbon."

the Cross writes, "I would not consider any spirituality worthwhile that wants to walk in sweetness and ease and run from the imitation of Christ."[21] In the Christian tradition, *theosis*, or partaking in the divine nature, starts with a self-emptying. Holy detachment is a kind of self-emptying; it starts with a right passion of mourning for the ways in which we're not like God. It's right to feel sorrow for the ways we've destroyed life and well-being in ourselves and those around us and, most particularly, for the separation from God that is the consequence of sin. As we've seen, the modern person attempts to discover their "authentic self" outside of conversation with God, which typically leads to exemplifying the false self—that self that seeks to win approval, to satisfy ego, to win at all costs. Thomas Merton comments that such people "try to become real by imposing themselves on other people, by appropriating for themselves some share of the limited supply of created goods and thus emphasizing the difference between themselves and other men who have less than they, or nothing at all."[22] In other words, modern people try to go within themselves by attempting to identify what makes them better than everyone else.

But the path of the authentic and true self is actually one of death by self-giving: "The renunciation of existing-for-oneself is man's most authentically personal act and so also man's most *Godlike* act."[23] Or as Thomas Merton posits, "To say that I am made in the image of God is to say that love is the reason for my existence, for God is love. Love is my true identity. Selflessness is my true self. Love is my true character. Love is my name."[24] To become divine, like Jesus, we empty ourselves of the passions that wage war within us and become nothing, so that, like Jesus, we can rise to life with God. The real authentic self is found in killing the alleged authentic self. Our ambition ceases as God becomes more in us.

Jesus compares transformation to a seed that goes into the ground to die so that it may rise to new life (John 12:24). But by being buried and dying, the seed becomes more like its true and ideal self, not

21. John of the Cross, *Dark Night of the Soul* 2.7.8 (Lewis, 97).
22. Merton, *New Seeds of Contemplation*, 47.
23. Williams, *Wrestling with Angels*, 14.
24. Merton, *New Seeds of Contemplation*, 60.

less so. The same is true with humanity. We need to be purged of ourselves to become our true, redeemed self. Being like God starts with emptying ourselves of our passions that strive for dominance or control or manipulation. It starts with detachment. Transformation requires death.

ILLUMINATION

The process of transformation doesn't end in death. If we stop at purgation, we become masochists. If we stop at purgation in the bourbon world, all we have is what distillers call "slop." The slop is nothing. Making the slop into something requires heat. In the next step the slop is heated to induce the evaporation process, leaving only the truest, most authentic form of the grain or corn. Distillers call what's left "white dog"—a pure and potent liquid.

Illumination is coming to know and become one's truest self, becoming comfortable in one's redeemed skin. Robert Farrar Capon puts it this way:

> It is Jesus who is your life. If he refused to condemn you because your works were rotten, he certainly isn't going to flunk you because your faith isn't so hot. You can fail utterly and still live the life of grace. You can fold up, spiritually, morally, or intellectually and still be sage. Because at the very worst, all you can be is dead—and for him who is the Resurrection and the Life, that just makes you his cup of tea.[25]

The heat of this realization creates an acceptance of the process that God is enacting. Dying is incomplete, but it's the first step. Many Christians undergoing this refinement process find a growing comfort in it. God is working with you to make you something. You are God's handiwork, *poiēma* (Eph. 2:10), created in Christ Jesus for good works.

UNION

The last step is union. The white dog must now sit in oak barrels for years. The barrels swell and shrink with the changing seasons.

25. Capon, *Between Noon and Three*, 292.

The wood expands under the humidity of Kentucky summers and contracts as winter winds blow. There's an organic breathing process that occurs. After each season, more and more liquid evaporates as the oak seeps into the bourbon, giving it its brown hue. After many years the union of white dog and barrel is complete. The swelling of barrels creates a union of substance. They bleed into each other.

Milliner, drawing on Merton, concludes the parallel between bourbon and spiritual transformation:

> "We must 'empty ourselves' as He did. We must 'deny ourselves' and in some sense make ourselves 'nothing' in order that we may live not so much in ourselves as in Him. We must live by a power and a light that seem not to be there. We must live by the strength of an apparent emptiness that is always truly empty and yet never fails to support us at every moment. This is holiness."
>
> Such is the paradox of bourbon: The less there is of it, the better. As a truly great bourbon reaches its peak, the amber liquid increases in richness, hue, and complexity while decreasing in quantity. The greatest sip of bourbon must therefore, necessarily, be the barrel's last solitary drop. Emptiness is perfection.[26]

As we pour ourselves out in service, as we become detached from ourselves and attached to God, as we become less ourselves and more like God, we become our finest selves. *Theosis* is complete. We become the completion subsumed in God.

CONCLUSION

The rock band Florence and the Machine filmed a music video in Ukraine in 2022, during that country's ongoing conflict with Russia. The song they perform in the video is called "Free." Following Florence around is an actor, who serves as a symbol of her anxiety. This actor controls her and is a constant presence and burden. Her emotion, she sings, "picks me up" and "puts me down a thousand times a day." She's seeking freedom, but she seems bound by her feelings.

26. Milliner, "Becoming Bourbon."

She reveals that some of her anxiety comes from living with the constant pressure of suffering and death. How is she supposed to keep singing with such raging emotions and anxieties? But she continues, "There's nothing else that I can do except to open up my arms and give it all to you." The identity of this "you" is ambiguous. But the song emerges from her anxieties, lifting her up and putting her down to the dancing refrain of "I am free." She leans her head up against her anxiety. She becomes friends with her feelings. The actor symbolizing anxiety puts her arm around Florence. Florence is the mountain. She notices the anxiety, yet she's free.

I think it's a beautiful picture of the things we've discussed in this chapter. Where attention to the self and urges for control can be all-consuming, holy detachment invites attention to different concerns—namely, to those things that concern God. It requires a contemplative purgation, which leads to union. This union is perfect freedom, a receptivity to the world rather than an imposition of power upon it in an attempt to manipulate and manufacture the things we want. God transforms our wants. In such a contemplation we are, like Florence, free.

✳ 9 ✳

TERESA of ÁVILA

EXPLORING THE INTERIOR CASTLE

I remember making fun of worship music when I was a graduate student. Perhaps because I heard criticisms from a professor or from classmates I wanted to fit in with, I thought individualistic worship songs seemed a bit too intimate. From "In the Garden," where Jesus "walks with me and talks with me and tells me I am his own," to "How He Loves," where David Crowder sings of heaven meeting earth "like a sloppy, wet kiss," there seemed to be a strain of music that sang of Jesus as if he were a boyfriend. In many of the songs I critiqued, Jesus seemed too personal, too sentimental. I wanted depth.

But based on the above chapters, don't these songs depict what we want? Shouldn't we desire such a close and intimate experience of Jesus that it feels like we're walking hand in hand in the garden? Don't we want to experience his presence that closely? True, I'm still not comfortable singing about sloppy, wet kisses. But the song has a right desire for intimacy with Jesus. The Song of Solomon is in the Bible, after all. Teresa of Ávila is one who desired such intimacy with Jesus.

THE LIFE OF SAINT TERESA

Teresa of Ávila is a refreshing female voice from a male-dominated medieval world. There aren't many female spiritual writers from this period for the simple fact that few women were educated or looked to for spiritual guidance. Born in March 1515 to a family of twelve children, she was raised in relative comfort and wealth. Teresa was beautiful and was a bit flirtatious as a young woman, to the consternation of her father. For the dual purpose of punishment and purification, he sent Teresa to a convent with Augustinian nuns for eighteen months. He may have lived to regret that decision. This time away proved to be decisive for Teresa. After returning home she left again in secret, not to rendezvous with a suitor but to enter the cloister. She took the habit in 1536.

Significant in her formation was a sickness in her early adult life. Through questionable medieval medical practice, Teresa entered a coma. For three years her mobility was limited—as was her prayer life. She would go on to say that this sickness affected her in such a way that she was unable to have an active and robust prayer life for ten years due to physical weakness. As was the case for many others, her early suffering shaped her life with God. She underwent her purgation.

Throughout her life she experienced powerful mystical visions with Jesus. While she was confident in her judgments of the true source of these revelations, she wasn't like a modern-age guru who claims infallibility. She was untrusting of her own experience and needed confessors to assure and stabilize her. For Teresa, intimacy with God was not a loner spirituality. She had several spiritual directors she would meet with to test these visions. Some of the directors doubted that the visions were from God and wondered whether they stemmed from a diabolical source. When she was unsure, she always submitted her experience to the judgment of others. She sought illumination.

In the modern world, nothing trumps an experience. Instead of *sola scriptura* (deriving doctrine from Scripture alone), the new standard is one's own experience alone. But for Teresa, even the most intimate sharing between friends was subject to criticism and scrutiny from others. She knew nothing of a "Lone Ranger" Christianity.

Teresa of Ávila was a critic of her own experience. She went on to help novices discern whether certain revelations or experiences were divine or diabolical, whether they should explore them or ignore them. She was all too aware of the deceits of the imagination and unreliability of people who wanted to stir up emotion or exploit a divine experience for personal gain.

During Teresa's life there was another movement that complicated her monastic ministry. Shortly after the Protestant Reformation, the Spanish church became a key scene in the Counter-Reformation, also called the Catholic Reformation. On top of this, the Spanish Inquisition was in force. Because of the influence of Protestants such as Martin Luther and John Calvin, some in the Catholic Church were suspicious of any new movements or individual calls for renewal. Renewal was how Luther's Reformation started, and Catholics were wary of any potential division. This situation affected Teresa because she was often misunderstood by or even thrown out of the communities she founded. She found herself assaulted with questions while she was trying to help, and these experiences led to deep pain, hurt, and confusion.

This pain was part of the purgation process. She entered dark nights and lonely days. Her will and ego had to be stripped before they could be filled with light. As Rowan Williams notes in his book on Teresa, "Yet she perseveres: finding that what God gives in prayer is quite disproportionate to her felt enthusiasm. God responds, not to the state of her emotions, but to the desire and direction shown in her life overall: to her knowledge of her neediness and fragmentation, not to any eagerness to acquire spiritual experiences."[1] For Teresa, prayer was driven by desire but not dictated by desire. She wanted intense experiences of God, but feelings were not the determining factor in whether a prayer time was valuable. She was driven by her neediness, and through her neediness God healed her.

A main theme emerges from the life of Saint Teresa: God overrules her selfish will. She realized her own fragmented and twisted desires, yet as in the life of Augustine, God used mixed motives and turned them straight. Just as God used Augustine's twisted ambition, he

1. Williams, *Teresa of Avila*, 51.

used Teresa's urge to be loved and admired.[2] God took this desire and turned Teresa toward himself. Being loved by God, she released her desire to be loved or accepted by everyone else, including by those involved in the Inquisition, who doubted her experience. The freedom she gained from being loved by Jesus saved her from any need to demand the respect of others.

DRIVING DESIRES: MOVEMENT WITHIN THE INTERIOR CASTLE

Her soul's quest started in desire, and her soul's rest ended with desire. On October 4, Teresa passed away while reciting lines from the Song of Songs and thanking God she was part of the church. Love for Jesus and love for the church were not competing desires for Teresa. Her intimate and individual experience of Christ never led to division from the church at large.

Gian Lorenzo Bernini's *Ecstasy of Saint Teresa*, a famous work of sculpture displayed in the Cornaro Chapel in Rome, displays the erotic nature of Teresa's desire. She looks up as an angel pierces her heart, golden sculpted rays shining upon the scene. Her face is pained, but the expression also could be interpreted as orgasmic or erotic. Teresa uses charged and provocative imagery in her writings that describe the nature of her intimacy with Jesus. In baroque fashion, Bernini's statue of "ecstasy" is passionate and evocative. The personal love of Jesus was that intense for Teresa. It is easy to see why some authorities of Teresa's day were uncomfortable! Yet she died quoting the Song of Songs, a book full of erotic imagery that can be read as analogous to God's love and desire for us.

For Teresa, the first step in prayer is the realization that God is very near and that harm comes from not understanding this continual close presence of God. In meditating on Christ she tempers reflections on the pain and love on display at the cross with the insistence that we should "rather stay there beside Him, with all our thoughts stilled. We should occupy ourselves, if we can, by gazing at Him who

---

2. Teresa refers to Augustine's *Confessions* and says that she saw herself in Augustine's story. Teresa, *Life of Saint Teresa of Avila* 9.7–8.

is gazing at us, should keep Him company, and talk with Him, and pray to Him, and humble ourselves and delight in Him, and remind ourselves that we do not deserve to be there."[3] What a beautiful description of prayer: gazing at him who is gazing at us. As we saw in chapter 8, attention and contemplation function the same way. Teresa desired this intimacy with and delight in Jesus, the beatific vision that transforms us. Gazing at Jesus results in humility, the first step in becoming like God in *theosis*.

In her most famous work, *The Interior Castle*, Teresa compares the soul to a precious jewel, "like a castle made entirely out of a diamond or of a very clear crystal, in which there are many rooms."[4] The work of spiritual formation takes us on a journey within the complex soul. So often, young people want to experience the world outside of themselves through travel and new experiences. To that, Teresa might say, "Try your soul first. There's plenty there to discover." *The Interior Castle* is a practical guide to the way the soul arrives at union with God through cooperation with grace. God was something to discover not outside but within. She writes, "We are to go inward, moving deeper and deeper into stillness and silence. If we travel to the center of the soul, there we encounter God."[5] On this note Rowan Williams proposes, "We enter the castle and, if our eyes are open, what we actually see is God, radiating love from the 'centre' which is the centre of our creatureliness. By seeing God we see more clearly what we are—muddled, distracted, frustrated, but in motion towards the love of God."[6] As we've seen, this dual knowledge of God and ourselves is a common theme in Christian spirituality. By entering the soul, we see God more clearly. By seeing God more clearly, we understand ourselves more truly.

Teresa goes on to describe the journey into the soul as a passage through seven different mansions. A commentator on Teresa, Shirley Darcus Sullivan, describes the purpose of her work: "Teresa suggests a process of growing more and more aware of what is truly

3. Teresa, *Life of Saint Teresa of Avila*, 96. I'm indebted to my friend Rebekah Linton, who pointed me to this passage.
4. Teresa of Avila, *Interior Castle*, 283.
5. Sullivan, *Transformed by Love*, 33.
6. Williams, *Teresa of Avila*, 149.

valuable. We move from attachment to lesser 'goods' to the highest good, God."[7] Teresa's process of contemplation is therefore also a process of holy detachment, learning to care about the things that God cares about. The division of the process into mansions is not supposed to provide a means of measuring one's progress. Rather, the mansions exist for self-reflection and for spiritual directors. The goal is to forget about the self and which mansion one is in. The purpose is the death of the ego (purgation) and ultimate union with God.

The first three mansions are somewhat reachable by human effort and striving. However, the remaining four are passive. They are mystical achievements and are granted by God alone. When starting out, we should expect a certain amount of dryness and a certain number of trials in our spiritual life. This stage can be compared to purgation. We may not experience consolations from God or find that our desires line up with God's desire. Even if he should offer us eternal delights, what makes us think that our desires would line up with God's delight? We need to be refined. Teresa advises,

> There's no need for us to be advising Him about what He should give us, for He can rightly tell us that we don't know what we're asking for. The whole aim of any person who is beginning prayer—and don't forget this, because it's very important—should be that he work and prepare himself with determination and every possible effort to bring his will into conformity with God's will.[8]

The key in these early stages is not to give up, even in dryness. Rather, we must be prompt in obedience regardless of feeling or even our own will because, as Teresa observes, "doing our own will is usually what harms us."[9] For Teresa, self-expression is overrated. We resign our will to the will of God, and the death of self-interest increases the pursuit of God. At each mansion there is a desire for more, as there was with Moses. Strivings end, and we begin to love God without self-interest. We grow from one degree of glory to another, never exhausting the intimacy that God gives.

7. Sullivan, *Transformed by Love*, 30.
8. Teresa of Ávila, *Interior Castle* 2.1.8 (Kavanaugh and Rodriguez, 43).
9. Teresa of Ávila, *Interior Castle* 3.2.12 (Kavanaugh and Rodriguez, 74).

Teresa compares the process of transformation to a silkworm turning into a moth. A silkworm, which she calls fat and ugly, toils and eats until it begins spinning a cocoon and enclosing itself. This is the work of the first three mansions. Our will, like the silkworm, prepares for its own binding and confinement. The work we do results in a rest during which something mysterious happens in the hidden resources of the spiritual cocoon. Teresa references Colossians 3, where Paul writes, "For you have died, and your life is hidden with Christ in God" (Col. 3:3). Death and hiding in Christ is the goal of the interior journey.

> Oh, then, my daughters! Let us hasten to perform this task and spin this cocoon. Let us renounce our self-love, and self-will, and our attachment to earthly things. Let us practice penance, prayer, mortification, obedience, and all the other good works that you know of. Let us do what we have been taught; and we have been instructed about what our duty is. Let the silkworm die—let it die, as in fact it does when it has completed the work which it was created to do. Then we shall see God and shall ourselves be as completely hidden in His greatness as is this little worm in its cocoon. Note that, when I speak of seeing God, I am referring to the way in which, as I have said, He allows Himself to be apprehended in this kind of union.[10]

The silkworm stops spinning when it realizes it can fly. Emerging from the cocoon is a beautiful moth. In the same way, knowing that creatures cannot give us rest, we realize that a life worth living is found in the Creator rather than in creatures. The appeal to find comfort and joy in the things of the earth loses its luster. We are no longer silkworms; we are moths. When we are detached from immature relationships and possessions, transformation occurs.

In the final and seventh mansion, Teresa ends a section like this: "I am laughing at myself over these comparisons for they do not satisfy me, but I don't know any others. You may think what you want; what I have said is true."[11] Basically, Teresa summarizes the final mansions with these words: "You have to be there to know what I mean." While this may leave some readers wanting more, that's the point, in a way.

10. Teresa of Ávila, *Interior Castle* 5.2.8 (Kavanaugh and Rodriguez, 148).
11. Teresa of Ávila, *Interior Castle* 7.2.11 (Kavanaugh and Rodriguez, 379).

For those who have developed close intimacy with God, words begin to fail. You have to be there to see. One finds mystery and awe, not explanations.

This pilgrimage into the soul is not a search for some authentic self, either. Self-awareness is how we begin the journey.[12] This awareness leads to divine absorption rather than self-absorption. True awareness is found in relation to God and thus requires humility and repentance. Teresa writes, "Mental prayer in my opinion is nothing else than an intimate sharing between friends; it means taking time frequently to be alone with Him who we know loves us."[13] The personal, inward experience drives us upward.

PRAY AND WORK

The intimacy that drives us upward also leads us outward. For Teresa, prayer leads to humility and then to service. One of Teresa's unique contributions is her idea of how the contemplative life necessarily leads people to love others. Earlier monastic writers tried to find characteristics of visionary experiences that would help them tell whether visions had to do with God. But not so with Teresa. Her intent is not to analyze the experience itself but to focus on the outcome of the experience—namely, one's behavior toward God and neighbor. She urges, "Let us desire and be occupied in prayer not for the sake of our enjoyment but so as to have this strength to serve."[14] If the experience fails to make a person more Christlike, then it fails to be a vision from God and is worthy of doubt.

Important to note is the centrality of honor in Teresa's society.[15] It would be natural for her to seek such honor; however, she is scathing in her critique of honor. She sees honor not as rooted in inherited status or in one's works. As she consistently notes, however, honor is interior. Once someone travels through the mansions and realizes

12. Teresa also makes the claim that self-knowledge is the first room to find, but regardless, self-awareness occurs toward the beginning of the soul's journey (*Interior Castle* 1.2.8–9).

13. Teresa, *Life of Saint Teresa of Avila* 8.5 (Cohen, 44).

14. Teresa of Ávila, *Interior Castle* 7.4.12 (Kavanaugh and Rodriguez, 412).

15. Rowan Williams, *Teresa of Avila*, 18–26.

the divine diamond within, they have every motive to treat others with honor and respect. God has made us his friends; therefore, we make friends with others, even if their class or spiritual maturity is different from ours. Teresa advocates for a countercultural love that sees the proper goal of spiritual maturity as love.

Such love is driven by humility. Teresa is worth quoting at length:

> While we are on this earth nothing is more important than humility. So I repeat that it is good, indeed very good, to try to enter the room where self-knowledge is dealt with rather than fly off to other rooms. This is the right road, and if we can journey along a safe and level path, why should we want wings to fly? Rather let's strive to make more progress in self-knowledge, for in my opinion we shall never completely know ourselves if we don't strive to know God. By gazing at His grandeur, we get in touch with our own lowliness; by looking at His purity, we shall see our own filth; by pondering His humility, we shall see how far we are from being humble.[16]

Teresa is adamant that we never deserve such visions and experiences. Growing in the mansions is not an expectation. Rather, we need to be obedient to what we receive. She clarifies, "Thus, the soul doesn't think about receiving more but about how to serve for what it has received."[17] In making this comment, Teresa urges us to a practical contemplation.

In Luke 10:25–37, Jesus tells a parable about a good Samaritan. We briefly looked at the parable in chapter 4. Eternal life is about loving our neighbor. This is what monastic spirituality has called the active life. Right after the Samaritan parable is a story about Mary and Martha (Luke 10:38–42).

Martha is being a good neighbor. She is attending to the household needs by offering hospitality. Mary, however, is attending to Jesus himself. Mary is identified by many writers as embodying the passive or contemplative life. Then Martha goes to Jesus and basically asks him, "Aren't you going to tell Mary to help?" Jesus answers, "Martha, Martha, you are anxious and troubled about many things,

16. Teresa of Ávila, *Interior Castle* 1.2.9 (Kavanaugh and Rodriguez, 24).
17. Teresa of Ávila, *Interior Castle* 6.9.16 (Kavanaugh and Rodriguez, 179).

but one thing is necessary. Mary has chosen the good portion, which will not be taken away from her" (Luke 10:41–42). In the Christian tradition the active and passive lives can often be seen in conflict with one another. From Jesus's words, it seems that the contemplative is the better lot.

The contemplative Teresa, however, suggests an organic link between mysticism and asceticism, passive and active life. You can't have one without the other. There is no mysticism without asceticism, or for the sake of this story, there is no Mary without Martha. In one letter, she writes to novices in the monastery who are seeking to be Marys rather than Marthas. "But my daughters, good heavens! Do not be disconsolate when obedience leads you to be concerned with external, worldly matters; understand that, if your task is in the kitchen, the Lord walks among the pots and pans, helping you in all things spiritual and temporal."[18] The contemplative life wasn't cause to leave the concerns of the world. It was cause to enter them more deeply, knowing that those were where God was already at work—"among the pots and the pans."

Traveling through the seven mansions is never the main point of life. Remember, there's only so much we can control, and we can never think we deserve greater revelations from God. The point is to be faithful with what has been revealed. The genuine experience of God makes the will of God easier to know and do, yet the experience is not necessary for obedience. Through trials and pain and through spiritual conversations, a person can choose God's will over their own, even without the aid of revelations. We're all called to be Martha, even if we never have the contemplative experience of Mary. The most important thing is to submit to the will of God, which is love.[19] To end *The Interior Castle*, Teresa commends building castles not in the air—some ethereal, prayerful, purely spiritual state—or on the greatness of our works but on "the love with which they [the works] are done."[20] Goodness and beauty aren't in competition. Rather, goodness prepares the way for a beautiful life of seeking the Beautiful One.

18. Teresa, *Book of the Foundations*, 31.
19. "The soul's progress does not lie in thinking much but in loving much" (Teresa, *Book of the Foundations*, 28).
20. Teresa of Ávila, *Interior Castle* 7.4.15 (Kavanaugh and Rodriguez, 415).

PRACTICES

CENTERING PRAYER

As discussed regarding the Jesus Prayer or returning to a word, the purpose of centering prayer is to be conscious of God's love in the present moment. Rather than saying words, centering prayer is what I have called a "sanctified shutting up." It's a passive way to pray, not to the total exclusion of words or petitions but as a deepening of them. It's a habit that helps us slow down and attend to God in the moment, to encounter him in silence.

SILENCE AND SOLITUDE

A goal of the beauty tradition is to be able to attend to God in the busy and noisy world, but we need some training in order to do that. Being quiet and alone helps us go deeper into our own souls, and as we saw with Teresa, this deepening also helps us discover God in the interior castle.

LECTIO DIVINA

Translated as "divine reading," *lectio divina* is an ancient way to read Scripture. Instead of focusing on the right answer or meaning, it helps us listen to the Spirit as we read. It's less about getting a theological insight and more about mining one's soul before the face of God. As Thomas Keating insists, "It is the savoring of the text, a leisurely lingering in divine revelation."[21] I appreciate this way of reading, as it exposes readers: you can't hide or pretend with *lectio divina*; you're confronted. What is the Holy Spirit saying to you today?

SABBATH

As Abraham Heschel notes, the first thing called holy in the Bible is time.[22] The Bible, he argues, is more concerned with time than with places. Practicing restful delight on the Sabbath trains us to *be* rather

21. Keating, *Intimacy with God*, 96.
22. Heschel, *Sabbath*, 7.

than to *do*, to be present rather than consume. Sabbath cultivates in us a contemplative spirit by habituating us to the holiness of time.

RESOURCES

Fujimura, Makoto. *Art and Faith: A Theology of Making*. New Haven: Yale University Press, 2020.

Laird, Martin. *Into the Silent Land: A Guide to the Christian Practice of Contemplation*. New York: Oxford University Press, 2006.

Merton, Thomas. *New Seeds of Contemplation*. New York: New Directions, 1961.

Underhill, Evelyn. *Mysticism: The Preeminent Study in the Nature and Development of Spiritual Consciousness*. New York: Doubleday, 1990.

PART 4

THE UNITED LIFE

LIVING IN COMMUNITY

The church is the primary presence of God's activity in the world. As we pay attention to what it means to be the church we create an alternative community to the society of the world. This new community, the embodied experience of God's kingdom, will draw people into itself and nurture them in the faith. In this sense the church and its life in the world will become the new apologetic.

—Robert Webber, *Ancient-Future Faith*

May the God of endurance and encouragement grant you to live in such harmony with one another, in accord with Christ Jesus, that together you may with one voice glorify the God and Father of our Lord Jesus Christ. Therefore welcome one another as Christ has welcomed you, for the glory of God.

—Romans 15:5–7

✳ 10 ✳

BELONGING TOGETHER

LONGING FOR COMMUNITY

In salvation history, the Lord saved one people. We are never completely ourselves unless we belong to a people. That is why no one is saved alone, as an isolated individual. Rather, God draws us to himself, taking into account the complex fabric of interpersonal relationships present in a human community. God wanted to enter into the life and history of a people.

—Pope Francis, *Gaudete et Exsultate*

We are utterly and desperately alone. At least, that's what life feels like for a lot of people. To quote Stanley Hauerwas again, the project of modernity is an "attempt to produce a people who believe that *they should have no story except the story that they choose when they had no story*."[1] We inherit nothing. We pass nothing on. This popular sentiment was clear in Taylor Swift's commencement address at New York University in 2022. She passed on this advice to the graduating seniors: "And I know it can be really overwhelming figuring out who to be, and when. Who you are now and how to act in order to get where you want to go. I have some good news: It's totally up to you.

---

1. Hauerwas, "End of American Protestantism."

I also have some terrifying news: It's totally up to you."[2] It's totally and eternally up to you. Good luck.

This loneliness and this rugged individualism have only grown with time. Robert Bellah and a team of researchers investigated how Americans viewed themselves in contemporary society, and their results were published in 1985.[3] The researchers identify two groups of self-understanding. They term the first group "utilitarian individuals." This group sees the goal of life as being successful, as moving up the social and economic ladder. These people can, and indeed must, improve by their own efforts alone. The world has competing interests, and people need to look out for their own, to pursue "success" no matter the cost. Whatever works. The second group of individuals are called "expressivist individuals."[4] The key to a good life is feeling good. That's really the only criterion. Material success is not as important as it is in the utilitarian mindset. Rather, the material aspects of life are valuable only to the extent that they lead to personal happiness. The measure of an activity or choice's worthiness is the pleasure that it brings the person. Whatever feels good. By and large, these are the two ways that Americans understand themselves and the two sets of values they use to make decisions. We are individuals through and through.

No one should be surprised, then, that Americans are also lonely and isolated. In a book published in 2000 called *Bowling Alone*, Robert Putnam tracks the loss of civic involvement in America. Whereas people used to join community clubs or groups, be involved in civic affairs, or join bowling leagues, now people "bowl alone." They don't join groups, but they take Taylor's advice: "It's totally up to you." More and more, Americans don't have friends to do activities with or to live alongside.

The impact of aloneness and isolation is the damage it does to social trust. We live in a story where we shouldn't trust others, and even if we wanted to trust others, we couldn't, since we don't know others very well. There is no one to trust. And these studies were published before smartphones were on the scene and social media

2. Dailey, "Taylor Swift's NYU Commencement Speech."
3. Bellah et al., *Habits of the Heart*, 32–33.
4. Bellah et al., *Habits of the Heart*, 34.

took off! The promise of connection has only put us in online echo chambers that hold the promise of real community but none of the benefits. Social isolation and fragmentation have only increased in the last twenty years.

Theologian Myles Werntz describes our modern times of self-making this way: we must "take on the burden of the world, carrying the weight of being self-made and self-sustained."[5] The crisis of anxiety among young people cannot be blamed simply on this type of rogue individualism, but the individualism sure can't help. Imagine going out into an uncertain world, being unsure of yourself and unsure of who to be or where to go, and knowing you can trust absolutely no one. That sounds more like terrifying news than good news to me.

The modern story that we have no story unless we choose a story when we have no story turns out to be a false story. Stanley Hauerwas argues that "to be a community which lives by remembering is a genuine achievement, as too often we assume that we can ensure our existence only by freeing ourselves from the past."[6] The church remembers. Church carries a narrative that confronts the world in which we live. Remembering is the church's witness.

In essence, you can't have part 1 of this book (truth) without community. To deny the church is to deny the communal narrative and to accept the individual narrative that you can choose your own story—and that you can carry that narrative to the next generation. But of course, if you live like this, you have no future generation to pass anything on to. The next generation should not listen to or trust you.

The true story is that we inherit a story and that we are intimately connected not only to others but also to place. We always see from someplace, and that fact doesn't need to be considered a limitation. It can be seen as a gift. We are unable to understand God apart from others or understand ourselves apart from others. We live mediated lives, gifted lives. We all came into being from two other people, and from our earliest beginnings we were dependent on parents who loved us into existence. We depend on others throughout our entire lives

5. Werntz, *From Isolation to Community*, 5.
6. Hauerwas, *Community of Character*, 68.

and will likely die in dependency on our children or on strangers. There's no getting around it. We are relational beings. I have good news: it's *not* totally up to you.

The world around us may say that each of us is utterly alone. But we need other people, and Jesus gifts us with those other people in the church. Spiritual formation is a group project.

THE STORY OF COMMUNITY IN THE BIBLE

Our relational life starts with the trinitarian life of God. Being made in God's image means being made in and for relational intimacy. Out of the trinitarian love of God—three persons in one essence—God creates. Before anything material existed, there was relational love.

When God creates, everything is good. After creating human beings, he looks back on all that he has made, and it is "very good" (Gen. 1:31). But God also notices something that is not good: the aloneness of man (2:18). So God makes a helper for Adam, a companion. When Adam discovers his helper, he sings a song. At last, someone fit for relationship.

But the relational intimacy does not last long. That serpent sneaks into the garden. First, he challenges their trust in God. "Did God actually say . . . ?" (Gen. 3:1). God can't be trusted. Humans must have the wisdom to trust themselves. When Adam and Eve take the fruit, they bear the fruit of their decision. Immediately, they hide. The intimacy they had with God has been broken. When God calls out to Adam, Adam blames Eve. He goes from singing a song, "bone of my bones and flesh of my flesh" (2:23), to "the woman whom you gave to be with me" (3:12). He throws Eve under the bus, even seeming to blame God for giving him the woman. The other is no longer a gift but a burden. Sin exiles humans from God and separates them from each other and from the land.

The vertical and horizontal fragmentation of relationship only intensifies throughout the biblical story. From the harmony of community in the garden, the story of brokenness and isolation spreads quickly. After the fall and exile from the garden, the next story we read is that of Cain and Abel (Gen. 4:1–16). Brothers, born to be companions, end up rivals. Cain kills Abel. When God asks Cain where his brother is—this question is reminiscent of God's question to Adam in Genesis 3:9—he responds, "Am I my brother's keeper?" (4:9). Individualism says the same thing: we can't be held responsible for other people.

Early civilizations come and work together on the tower of Babel (Gen. 11:1–9), which seems like good news. They are doing community building! But they use their relational connection to build a name for themselves. Their pride results in a break in intimacy with God, so God scatters the people and gives them different languages. Now the ways people speak are a further source of separation between them.

The story of Israel is the story of a continual fracturing of relationships. God chooses and blesses a people, not a loose gathering of individuals. His call to Israel is to be a people, "a kingdom of priests and a holy nation" (Exod. 19:5–6). He chooses different representatives to be leaders over his one people. But each leader lets the people down, from Abraham to Moses to David. God said the seed of Eve would crush the head of the serpent (Gen. 3:15), but this seed seems elusive. No one can be trusted. All there seems to be is relational dysfunction.

In the fullness of time Christ enters the scene in dependence. He needs the womb and nurture of a mother. It's really an astonishing fact: the omnipotent, self-sustaining God has come to earth as a dependent. The God who made everything has come into the world he made to be cared for and sustained by his own creatures. Christ's mission is to be a representative leader and to make a new people. The communal implications of Christ's accomplishment are clear in Ephesians 2:

> Therefore remember that at one time you Gentiles in the flesh, called "the uncircumcision" by what is called the circumcision, which is made in the flesh by hands—remember that you were at that time separated from Christ, alienated from the commonwealth of Israel and strangers to the covenants of promise, having no hope and without God in the world. But now in Christ Jesus you who once were far off have been brought near by the blood of Christ. For he himself is our peace, who has made us both one and has broken down in his flesh the dividing wall of hostility by abolishing the law of commandments expressed in ordinances, that he might create in himself one new man in place of

the two, so making peace, and might reconcile us both to God in one body through the cross, thereby killing the hostility. (Eph. 2:11–16)

We "who once were far off have been brought near." Christ broke down the dividing wall and made peace, reconciling us through the cross and killing the hostility between God and humans and also among humans. We hated God and each other, but in Christ we've become reconciled to God and each other.

Having been thus reconciled, "we are ambassadors for Christ, God making his appeal through us." We announce to the world, "Be reconciled to God" (2 Cor. 5:20). God is up to this cosmic reconciliation and restoring of relationship. His desire is to heal the relational divide between God and humanity, between each of us, and even within our fragmented selves.

The picture of the end of time that God presents is a picture of a new community. Thousands upon thousands, more people than can be counted, "from every nation, from all tribes and peoples and languages" are around the throne of God and are worshiping him (Rev. 7:9). People of different colors and languages and interests and nations will be reconciled to one another. Nations that warred against each other will be friends. All things will be put right. All relationships will be reconciled. All hurts will be healed.

THE CHURCH: A NEW PEOPLE (OR, BEYOND INDIVIDUALISM)

To say "Jesus is a King" implies he has a people. There is no people-less king. Jesus is ruling over his people, the church, and we together seek to submit to the lordship of King Jesus. In other words, the gospel does not involve only individual submission to Jesus; the gospel comes with profound communal implications for us as a people.

At the very beginning of the church, the gospel comes with power, and this power forms a community. In Acts 2, after Jesus ascends to heaven, the disciples gather and pray. And suddenly, with the sound of rushing wind, the Holy Spirit falls like tongues of fire. Diverse people from all over the world, who are gathered in Jerusalem, hear the gospel and testimony in their own tongue (vv. 1–13). Theologians call this a reversal of Babel. In Genesis 11 people were united in language, building a community to their own glory, but then the languages were confused and the people scattered. Now, in Christ, the language barriers are overcome and the people regathered so they can build a community for God's glory. God is building a transnational and multilingual community.

After the Spirit falls on the community of faith, Peter stands up—this Peter who denied Jesus just some fifty days earlier. He begins testifying to people who have the power to kill him. In addition to empowerment by the Spirit, the reality of the resurrection and ascension of Jesus gives Peter a confidence to witness despite the possibility of death (Acts 2:14–36). After hearing the truth of the gospel, the people respond, "What shall we do?" Peter says, "Repent and be baptized" (vv. 37–38). This baptism is into the trinitarian name of God, into a community of belonging. These new believers are baptized into a people.

Elsewhere, Peter relates baptism to Noah's ark (1 Pet. 3:20–21). There is a difference between Noah building an ark and God saving individuals on separate boats, a difference between a community and a collection of individuals. God saves humans from individualism, making them into a people. After the baptisms in Acts 2, the early church begins gathering consistently and even holding their possessions in common (Acts 2:42–47). There is no such thing as a lone or individual Christian in the early church. Conversion results in community.

The rest of Acts is a testimony of how this strange group of people in the power of the Holy Spirit grows throughout the ancient world. The start of the church in Philippi is a microcosm of the church reconciling a diverse people so that rich and poor, old and young, Jew and gentile gather around a common table. The Holy Spirit gives Christians a radical and sacrificial love for one another that crosses barriers of class, ethnicity, social status, and any other worldly difference.

In Acts 16:11–15 a rich woman named Lydia comes to faith in Jesus. Lydia is a seller of purple goods. Perhaps we could compare her to a successful fashion designer today. Paul goes down to a gathering of women, and while he is speaking the gospel truth, the Lord opens Lydia's heart to pay attention to what Paul is saying. She is converted, and she begs Paul and his companions to stay with her. The first disciple from Philippi that we know of responds to the gospel not just with faith in Jesus but with hospitality. Jesus welcomes her, and she welcomes others.

In the next scene (Acts 16:16–24), Paul and Silas are on their way to a prayer meeting when a demon-possessed slave girl starts shouting at them. Paul, as one could imagine, gets annoyed as this girl follows them around for days and constantly shouts at them, "These men are servants of the Most High God, who proclaim to you the way of salvation" (v. 17). That seems like free publicity, but after several days it gets old—perhaps like hearing a child saying "Dad, Dad, Dad" over and over. Paul commands the demon to come out of the slave girl, and her owners get mad, as they were raking in money from the girl's demonic witchcraft practice. So these men complain to the town officials, and Paul and Silas are beaten and taken to prison.

The third scene (Acts 16:25–40) tells of Paul and Silas in prison at midnight. If it were me, I'd be saying, "This is how you treat me, God? This is your faithfulness and goodness? I leave my religion and all my friends. I come to this foreign city. I'm trying to do your work by preaching the gospel. A rich lady is converted. A slave girl is converted. And this is my payback? Beaten and thrown in prison?" But that's not how Paul and Silas respond. They're not even sleeping at midnight. They're praying and singing hymns to God in their persecution. Then an earthquake occurs. The doors open, and the chains unfasten. The jailer is on the point of suicide, because if all the prisoners get out, he's dead. He might as well do it himself. But Paul shouts out, "Do not harm yourself, for we are all here" (v. 28). Instead of seeing this miracle as an invitation for escape, Paul sees it as an invitation for ministry. The jailer comes out and asks, "What must I do to be saved?" (v. 30). Paul repeats the salvation formula: Repent and be baptized. So, they go to the jailer's house and baptize his family.

Imagine this first church in Philippi. There is a rich lady, a high-class citizen who is well connected. There is a slave girl who's a former witch. She has been abused all her life and is likely needy because she has been in need and dependence her whole life. And we have a blue-collar jailer who's an agent of state occupation.

In many ways these people have always been used for what they could provide but have never been truly cared for or loved. Lydia, I imagine, was used for her connections and wealth. The girl with divination was discarded as soon as she was no longer profitable. The jailer's immediate response was to kill himself when the doors were opened. They're all insecure in their own ways because they don't know what it means to be fully known and truly loved.

And I'm sure each could be annoying in their own way too. "Lydia, enough with the purple clothes and the name-dropping. We know you're wealthy." Or "Could the slave girl be a bit more independent?" And "The jailer, he seems disconnected, emotionally distant, a loner."

What could possibly keep this diverse set of people together? How in the world is this early church going to survive? What hope does the church have with this ragtag bunch? What would keep these people loving and committed to each other?

In Jesus's last words before the cross, he gives us his plan. It's part of his prayer in John 17, called the High Priestly Prayer. Jesus offers his final prayer before heading to the cross. He prays for himself and his task, for his disciples, and for those who will come to believe in Jesus. Here's the central theme of his prayer: unity. His final prayer, spoken as his parting words to his disciples, is that they would be unified. And the way unity happens is through love.

Jesus prays, "I made known to them your name, and I will continue to make it known, that the love with which you have loved me may be in them, and I in them" (John 17:26). What an astonishing thought. The love with which God the Father loves God the Son can reside in those who will come to believe in Jesus. That means that if you believe in Jesus, you have access to the love with which the Father loves the Son. The never-ending, incomprehensible, inexhaustible, fervent, affectionate love of God resides within you, so you can love those around you—not just friends you choose but also the diversity of people in your church, people who sit around you and whom you may hardly know.

So the hope of the church of Philippi is the hope of the church at large. You are called together as different, strange, sometimes needy, sometimes angry people. Your church likely has conservatives and liberals, rich and poor, NRA members and pacifists, Black people and white people, employees and employers, homeless people and rooted people, emotional people and intellectual people. If all these people are put together in any other context, they may have no reason to be friends. Sometimes you may be a little embarrassed by fellow church members, and they may be embarrassed by you. You may even be enemies.

However, "God's love has been poured into our hearts" (Rom. 5:5), and now you have Jesus in common. And if you have the love of Jesus in common, then you have more than enough to remain united despite all that may tear the world apart. Those fleshly boundaries mean nothing to the church of Christ.

So the world ought to look in on the church and ask the same question that must have been asked around Philippi: "What do these people have in common? How in the world could they love each other?" And the answer is that Jesus keeps the church together, so its members don't need to have anything else in common in order to love each other. Stanley Hauerwas says, "The church is constituted as a new people who have been gathered from the nations to remind the world that we are in fact one people. Gathering, therefore, is an eschatological act as it is the foretaste of the unity of the communion of the saints."[7] Even when it seems like the church is fragile and divided, we continually meet to live into the unity and community that God has started and that God will complete.

THE LORD'S SUPPER AS COMMUNAL CONNECTION

In a traditional liturgy, as we prepare for the Lord's Supper, a member from the congregation brings the bread and wine to the table. It's a symbolic gesture showing that the gifts we offer the Lord are the gifts that God has already given us. We're returning the gifts God has given us. God's graciousness is shown to the world in his giving us gifts of wheat and grapes. Our creative gifts of cultivation turn the raw materials into bread and wine, and we then give back to God the bread and wine, a collective sacrifice of praise and thanksgiving. God, in turn, gives us the mysterious presence of his Son in and through the elements.

7. Hauerwas, *In Good Company*, 161.

Not only are the elements taken from the people, but the elements themselves connect us to one another. In a unique way, the Lord's Supper functions with communal underpinnings. A sermon can be interpreted individually. A song may touch one person and not another. The Lord's Supper, by contrast, is a common experience and communal practice. Many churches offer the wine in a single large cup. The symbolism is intentional. We don't have individual cups; we partake together from the one Christ. We eat and drink together as we share Christ's nourishment of grace. As Dietrich Bonhoeffer, who is the subject of chapter 12, suggests, in the Eucharist "Christ's presence means community with God through Christ and realization of the church-community as the bearer of individuals."[8] The Eucharist entails a mutual dependence.

On any occasion, eating together is formative. Sharing a meal is meaning-making. It's an opportunity to enjoy conversation and be grateful. At the Lord's Supper, all our shared meals find their ultimate meaning. All meals are symbolic representations of this perfect meal as we look forward to the marriage supper of the Lamb at the end of time—where people of all nations and languages will gather around a table to share a meal in eternity.

CONCLUSION

Community is the outflowing of our life with God. If we aim at community, we strangle community. We crush it by our expectations of what we think it should be. But if we aim at spiritual formation, we get community thrown in.

Life with God is like a team sport. If we take up a sport for the purpose of having friends, then we'll likely not be very good. And when trials and conflicts (and losses) come, there will be no rootedness and stability. We can get friends more easily someplace else. But if we aim to be excellent participants, then we'll have a lot more fun playing (and winning). We'll form deep bonds through sacrifice and mutual dependence. The friendships will be deeper than they would have been if we had joined for the sake of friendship.

8. Bonhoeffer, *Sanctorum Communio*, 243.

Spiritual formation functions in a similar way. We can choke friendships by the pressure we place on them if we focus on relationships in themselves. However, if we focus on growing with God, the outcome is a depth of community that strengthens and deepens us.

❊ 11 ❊

The WEB of EXISTENCE

COSMIC CONNECTIONS

Jayber Crow, the novel by Wendell Berry that I mentioned in chapter 7, portrays a character named Jayber in the small town of Port William, Kentucky. Typical of Berry, it's a slow-moving but profound book, following Jayber as he works as the town barber for over fifty years. Jayber is orphaned as a young boy, and the beginning of the story is about Jayber's resistance to dependence and constraint. He wants to be autonomous. Yet his quest for independence takes him to a town where he belongs, to a community that feels like family and fills the absence he's always felt. Port William takes Jayber in, as imperfect as the place is. He is viewed as suspect by some of the townspeople for being an aging bachelor, and he's judged by others for his chosen profession. But he becomes embedded in this web of existence. He has a role to play and a duty to fulfill, and by cutting hair, he comes to know the people and the rhythms of that place. He's entangled and cannot be independent. He comes to recognize the "normal" that can be known only locally and with time. He becomes part of the history of the place, and it begins to feel like home. He stops trying to figure out what he is going to be or where he is going to go. He settles in place.

At one point in the novel, Jayber shuts his eyes and imagines all the people of Port William, these people whom he has observed, judged, fought with, and loved. As he imagines this web of connection, "They were just there. They said nothing, and I said nothing. I seemed to love them all with a love that was mine merely because it included me. When I came to myself again, my face was wet with tears."[1] By committing to place, he has grown to love a people. He isn't like Troy, whom I mentioned before. Troy is restless, always wanting more, always pursuing the next big thing. Jayber settles on love, and love requires mutual sacrifice and the end of freedom. As David Brooks mentions in a college commencement address, "The things you chain yourself to set you free."[2] There's a deeper freedom that arises with commitment. Faith requires fidelity.

These cosmic connections are true for all of us. We have invisible roots that go down into webs of communion beneath the surface. Affection roots us in place, allowing the web to grow stronger and more durable.

In the first section of this chapter, I discuss the fundamental web of communion as found in the church. To be a Christian is to be part of a church community. In the second section of the chapter, I expand our connectedness beyond church members to neighbors. We are called to nourish the people and places that have nourished us.

LIVING INTO THE CHURCH

You need to commit to a local church. If you're like me, every element of that sentence makes you uncomfortable. A statement about me needing to do something is a nonstarter. It assumes someone has the authority to tell me what to do. And I don't like authority. Obedience implies a restriction on freedom, a disfiguring of who I am, because who I am is what I desire. And if I can't have my desire, then I can't truly be myself.

Myles Werntz argues that "to have *no* authority is to designate each individual an authority over their fragment of the world."[3] No

1. Berry, *Jayber Crow*, 165.
2. Brooks, "Ultimate Spoiler Alert."
3. Werntz, *From Isolation to Community*, 169.

authority is the way we like it. Hauerwas's critique of the modern project of meaning-making makes sense if we have no authority. We have no story until we choose a story. No one can tell me which story to choose. I inherit nothing. I'm an individual choosing my way and ruling over my fragment of the world.

The problem is that we want all the benefits of community with none of the requirements. Or as Ronald Rolheiser has written, "Typical today is the person who wants faith but not the church, the questions but not the answers, the religious but not the ecclesial, and the truth but not obedience."[4] We want community with no strings attached, no mutual commitment to one another. We desire a community that's easy to enter and easier to leave, with choices and no responsibility. In essence, we want a community void of all necessary elements of belonging.

The second problem after authority is commitment. No one likes commitments. Personally, I have a serious case of FOMO (fear of missing out). Commitments, like authority, limit my freedom of choice. I don't even like to commit to plans for a Friday night in case something better comes up. Commitments are scary. Moreover, it's easy in the modern world to throw things away rather than repair them. If a phone is old, buy the latest version. If a marriage is broken, get a new one. Moving up means moving on. Bigger is better. So if a community is broken (and what community isn't?), it seems easier to move on. Rather than working with what we have, we leave for some hopeful, better future.

But the church is a place of commitment. There are good reasons to leave a church—for instance, a dysfunctional or unhealthy church leadership or an intriguing opportunity in another city. But I think our overall tendency should be to stay. In a documentary called *Godspeed*, a film about slowing down our pace of life and getting to know neighbors in a parish sense, there's an interview with a monk. Benedictine monks take a vow of stability, promising to stay in the same monastery their whole life. In our mobile and global age, I know that sounds unthinkable. No travel? No exploration? Just stuck in the same spot? Yes. For these monks, commitment to place is a spiritual matter.[5]

4. Rolheiser, *Holy Longing*, 35.
5. Saint Anthony was once asked, "What must one do in order to please God?" "He replied, "Pay attention to what I tell you. Whoever you may be, always have God before your eyes. Whatever you do, do it according to the testimony of the holy

The monk who is interviewed, Father Giles, says the secret to stability is the realization that one is a sinner but a beloved sinner. He says, "Very quickly, you see people's faults. Look at that guy. But to see people's virtues, it takes longer. To learn to know takes time." He explains that modern culture may be obsessed with the "shallow novelty" of new experience, but deep relationship takes time. Later, he talks about growing with these brothers in place as an opportunity to see the grace of God at work. "You see Brother So and So. You can't get within two miles of him." But after ten years you can get within a single mile. And after twenty years a half mile. And after forty years maybe six feet. And if God can do that, what graces may he have at work within me?

Often, when a conflict occurs in my life, I am quick to leave. If a leader makes a decision I don't like, I'll go someplace else. Or if that lady seems arrogant and rude, I'll think that this isn't the right church for me. Or those guys seem closed off and distant, so let's get out of here. I can choose to live like that, but if I do I'll never stay anyplace long enough to truly know a people, and therefore I can never really love anyone or receive love in return. Worse, I'll never stay long enough to see the grace of God at work. Wendell Berry suggests we should carry forgiveness like a fire extinguisher. "If two neighbors know that they may seriously disagree, but that either of them, given even a small change of circumstances, may desperately need the other, should they not keep between them a sort of pre-paid forgiveness? They ought to keep it ready to hand, like a fire extinguisher."[6] The problem of many communities is that we live like we don't need one another. We think we can move on and not care. We don't live with affection, and we therefore have no prepaid forgiveness.

A life committed to stability requires radical honesty, truthfulness with one another in church.[7] The typical way I handle conflict is to

---

Scriptures. Wherever you live, do not easily leave it. Keep these precepts and you will be saved" (quoted in *Sayings of the Desert Fathers*, 2). Those first two pieces of advice are standard enough. But that third one hits the modern person differently. Anthony doesn't say never to move, but he does say not to leave easily. I think that's rich advice to heed in today's world. (And thanks to Ryan Smith for pointing me to this passage.)

6. Wickenden, "Wendell Berry's Advice for a Cataclysmic Age."

7. Truthfulness and honesty are a major emphasis for community life in Christine Pohl's *Living into Community*, 61–159.

bury my feelings deep down and never bring it up. I'll just wait till I feel better. But this way of handling conflict results in a false peace. The work of true peace requires daily mending. Mending is the work of love. On this note the novelist James Baldwin challenges me:

> If you do love somebody . . . you try to correct the person whom you love. Now that's a two-way street. You've also got to be corrected. . . . If I love you, I have to make you conscious of the things you don't see. . . . I will not see without you, and vice versa, and you will not see without me. No one wants to see more than he sees. You have to be driven to see what you see. The only way you can get through it is to accept that two-way street which is called love.[8]

The thing about blind spots is that you can't see them. So you need a community to help you see yourself more truly and pursue Jesus. In our right minds, don't we want people to help us forsake sin and pursue righteousness? If there's an obstacle to loving Jesus, don't we want that pointed out? Love is the commitment that we will sharpen one another and not run away when things get tough.

Here's the reality: We each contribute, positively or negatively, to a community of faith. We all make daily deposits, so to speak. Either our commitments and rhythm of life enrich a community, or our presence poisons it. Living in trivial, superficial, or restless ways poisons the stream of communal life. Commitment, by contrast, restores and nourishes a community.

This requirement to commit pertains to a particular local church, not to church in the abstract. The normal mode of being a Christian is going to a place where Christians gather together.[9] This commitment is harder than the commitment to the idea of church, since people have warts and idiosyncrasies. They are harder to love than

8. Baldwin, "*The Black Scholar* Interviews James Baldwin," 155–56.

9. The problem of "digital community" "begins with the scattering of people from one another as the default ground to which our vision of church then must be calibrated. When we construct church in such a way that all of the activities of the church can be fully and completely performed through our own individual thoughts, our own individual agency, our own individual interpretation mediated through our personal digital device, then what we are doing may very well be religiously informative or inspirational, but we will be accommodating to the conditions of isolation, not operating in defiance of them" (Werntz, *From Isolation to Community*, 34).

a vague sense of community. I've worked in the church for most of my adult life. I know how poorly people can be treated. I know how lousy life in church can be. I know what it's like to be embarrassed by people who are supposed to be like brothers and sisters but who act like weird, distant uncles. Communities are messy, worship can be emotionally manipulative, sermons can be shallow or boring or partisan, and so on. The list could go on. There are unhealthy dynamics at play. But as one Russian Christian says, "You're not a Christian so that you can be happy, you're not in the Church to be happy but to be alive."[10] When Jesus asks the disciples if they want to leave, Peter responds, "Lord, to whom shall we go? You have the words of eternal life" (John 6:68). I know the church can be messy, but Jesus gives the church, the body of Christ, stewardship of the words of eternal life. Where else could we go?

In the Roman Catholic tradition, there is a teaching that says: outside the church there is no salvation.[11] That may be uncomfortable to individualistic Protestant ears. Protestants broke away from what they considered to be a dysfunctional and lax church for greater purity, not less! However, even the early Reformer John Calvin teaches something similar. Citing the church father Saint Cyprian, who says we can't have God as Father without church as mother, Calvin writes, "But as it is now our purpose to discourse of the visible church, let us learn, from her single title of Mother, how useful, no, how necessary the knowledge of her is, since there is no other means of entering into life unless she conceive us in the womb and give us birth, unless she nourish us at her breasts, and, in short, keep us under her charge and government. . . . Moreover, beyond the pale of the church no forgiveness of sins, no salvation, can be hoped for."[12] Commitment to Christ entails commitment to a church. There is no other way of salvation, as we saw in Acts. The way we enter the church is by being baptized and taking on the trinitarian name of the Father, Son, and Holy Spirit. Only the church has the authority to baptize in the name of God. No one has the authority to call themselves a

10. A Russian Christian as quoted in Williams, *Looking East in Winter*, 158.
11. See Espín and Nickoloff, *Introductory Dictionary of Theology and Religious Studies*, 439.
12. Calvin, *Institutes of the Christian Religion* 4.1.4 (Beveridge, 674).

Christian. They can say the words, but baptism is the proof. In the same way, someone could say they're funny. We'll see about that. In baptism the church gives the stamp of approval—yes, this person is who they say they are.

THE COMPELLING COMMUNITY

The power of Christian witness depends upon the quality of our life together. Love is the sign that we are Christ's disciples (John 13:35). A lack of love, which sometimes characterizes Christian congregations, is antithetical to the gospel. Christine Pohl affirms, "The beauty of loving communities does not replace the importance of the verbal proclamation of the gospel, but Jesus explicitly linked the truth of his life and message to our life together."[13] The outworking of the gospel is love overflowing from the community into the world.

In the fourth century, Saint Basil of Caesarea was elected as a bishop in the church. Coming from a wealthy and connected family, he had all the means necessary to be "successful." Yet he gave up all his privilege to serve the poor. During his time as bishop, a great famine arose in Caesarea that caused many impoverished people to become even more destitute. Many in the city underwent a slow and terrible death by starvation. Basil got to work. He preached sermons condemning money lenders and the rich. He recognized the institutional injustices that faced the poor. He would preach things like this:

> Who is a man of greed? Someone who does not rest content with what is sufficient. Who is a cheater? Someone who takes away what belongs to others. And are you not a man of greed? Are you not a cheater? Taking those things which you received for the sake of stewardship, and making them your very own? Now, someone who takes a man who is clothed and renders him naked would be termed a robber; but when someone fails to clothe the naked, while he is able to do this, is such a man deserving of any other appellation? The bread which you hold back belongs to the hungry; the coat, which you guard in your locked storage-chests, belongs to the naked; the footwear mouldering in your closet belongs to those without shoes. The silver that you

13. Pohl, *Living into Community*, 2.

keep hidden in a safe place belongs to the one in need. Thus, however many are those whom you could have provided for, so many are those whom you wrong.[14]

Saint Basil didn't play around. He convicts us of complacency and greed.

Basil's lasting impact was establishing what came to be known as *basileas*, which translates into "new cities." They were to be places of hospitality for the poor, serving as both a home and a hospital. *Basileas* also provided vocational training so that the poor could contribute to the needs of others as well as seek employment.[15] Foundational to Basil's ministry was meeting the needs of others. His monasticism included activism. He cared about both spiritual and material needs.

Basileas found expression several centuries later in Celtic spirituality. George Hunter III details the difference between Roman and Eastern monastic communities, on the one hand, and Celtic monastic communities, on the other. Whereas the Eastern monasteries were formed to protest the materialism of the Roman world and the corruption in the church, Celtic monasteries were "organized to penetrate the pagan world and to extend the Church."[16] It was a movement not of escapism but of missional strategy. Hunter continues, "The wall [of the monastery] did not signify an enclosure to keep out the world; the area signified the 'alternative' way of life, free of aggression and violence and devoted to God's purposes, that the community modeled for the world."[17] These walls were not exclusionary but opened to hallowed ground—an alternative community that lived in alternative ways. Celtic spirituality therefore produced ways of living that were more communal than the individualistic or tribal lifestyles that surrounded them. The people of their monasteries lived in contact with place and the ground and cultivated the earth as they cultivated one another. Their beautiful setting impacted the way they lived on the land, close to nature.

14. Basil the Great, *On Social Justice*, 69.
15. See Smither, *Mission in the Early Church*, 137–38.
16. Hunter, *Celtic Way of Evangelism*, 28.
17. Hunter, *Celtic Way of Evangelism*, 29.

In living with distinct rhythms, the church offers a compelling welcome to the outside world. There is distinction—this is the church, and this is the world—yet the church always has its arms open. We know what it's like to be welcomed as a stranger because Christ has welcomed us. Therefore, we welcome the strangers among us. Christians are distinct in the way they love each other, so onlookers see a community where people truly love, forgive, and serve one another, unlike people in the broader community. A Christian community should be the tangible reality of the love and community that the outside world has always longed for but never knew existed.

HOW TO TELL TIME AND HOW TO LIVE: THE LITURGICAL YEAR

My wife and I were both raised in religiously apathetic homes. Perhaps you could call us both cultural Catholics—my wife being of the Hispanic variety and me being of the Italian variety. We went to church sometimes, but church life was never a commitment that defined us. Church was not a story we carried or desired but was more something we were coerced into. I can't remember a religious conversation from my childhood. That does not mean they did not happen, but spirituality did not seem to be an animating force for our family.

When my wife and I started a family, tradition was hard for us. It felt like we did not have any. How do we organize a family and establish rhythms? What traditions should our kids have? What do we do for Christmas? Or Easter? How do we spiritually form our children? Should we fast for Lent? It was all fair game. So many choices with no direction can be debilitating for people making decisions. It all felt so consequential, but we had no wise guides to help us. How do I make up practices that will help and not harm my children? How do I know what works? What do I want to pass on to future generations? What has worked in the past? I did not have the resources to answer these questions.

I realized that taking up spiritual practices is a lot easier in community. I'm not strong enough by myself or in my family unit to succeed at spiritual formation. I need others with me, encouraging me, helping me, guiding me.

Tradition helped ballast me. Tradition may seem stifling and archaic, but every community, and every family, has traditions. Tradition helps us live into the world by taking up practices of the past. The church is not an information-transfer station but training for a way of life. To help assist people in living in the world, the church gives us a calendar that tells time differently than the popular culture does. Myles Werntz notes, "Our lives are not just a litany of activities to be accomplished but an ordering of time that must be reclaimed."[18] Time is told in certain ways. If you're a student, your time is ordered from August to May. If you're an accountant, the crunch of tax season is in April. If you've been formed by American culture, the year starts at New Year's Day and proceeds through Valentine's Day, Easter, Mother's Day, and a few other special days until it arrives at its climax: consumer Christmas.

In a provocative talk at a youth conference, Stanley Hauerwas challenged the upcoming generation.

> I assume most of you are here because you think you are Christians, but it is not at all clear to me that the Christianity that has made you Christians is Christianity. For example:
>
> —How many of you worship in a church with an American flag? I am sorry to tell you your salvation is in doubt.
> —How many worship in a church in which the Fourth of July is celebrated? I am sorry to tell you your salvation is in doubt.
> —How many of you worship in a church that recognizes Thanksgiving? I am sorry to tell you your salvation is in doubt.
> —How many of you worship in a church that celebrates January 1st as the "New Year"? I am sorry to tell you your salvation is in doubt.
> —How many of you worship in a church that recognizes "Mother's Day"? I am sorry to tell you your salvation is in doubt. . . .
>
> I have not made the claims above to shock you, but rather to put you in a position to discover how odd being a Christian makes you.[19]

18. Werntz, *From Isolation to Community*, 93.
19. Hauerwas, *Working with Words*, 116–17.

Though I may not put it as bluntly as Hauerwas does, I agree with the point he is making. Christians have a different culture and therefore a different way of telling time. Indeed, the way people tell time is one shaping feature of a culture. Rabbi Abraham Heschel argues that Judaism creates an architecture of time.[20] If the same God of Israel gave them a culture-shaping calendar full of tradition and holy days and practices, why would he change plans with the church? Isn't it just as important for the church today to pass on a distinct culture as it was for Judaism then? We still tell time, and God has a way of sanctifying time. God is still at work in making a people, not individual monads.

One of the gifts of the church calendar is the opportunity to remind ourselves that time is not a commodity that is running out but is rather a gift to celebrate. As I mentioned in chapter 7, in my own life I can feel like I'm chasing after productivity, striving to make the most of my time. The ancient church comes to me to say, "Stop." Rather than grasp the limited resource of time, I'm invited to accept time as a gift. "You're in this rhythmic year. It's here now. There's a season. Live into it. This time will come again." Each year, I experience the same events differently—I've grown, changed, reached a different place in life. Each season is different because I'm passing through it a different person, and I see something new each time through. Time is like a spiral leading us and maturing us as we "fall upward."[21] The calendar orients me to the world in a different way. It's a cyclical calendar rather than a linear life. The weekly and yearly liturgy ("the work of the people") is the primary place that cultivates a Christ-consciousness in time. The church can slow us down so that we see.[22] The world disorders us, and we need the church to reorder us.

You may be overwhelmed hearing about all these practices. By the end of the book, I'll have given you sixteen practices—and that's a condensed list. There are more! I remember being overwhelmed when

20. Heschel, *Sabbath*, 8.
21. See Rohr, *Falling Upward*. Rohr uses the phrase to refer to the way in which failures in "the second half of life" can lead to spiritual growth.
22. Much could be said about the church becoming a distraction station and playing into the temptation to be an entertainment factory. If we value the principles of the world, there's no wonder the church does not have much formative power.

introduced to spiritual formation. How am I supposed to read the Bible, pray, memorize Scripture, do contemplative exercises, fast, and feast? And do I do these things every day? At the same time? In every season? Of course, the answer to these last three questions is no. The practices need to be distributed. Coming up with an original way to distribute them can be overwhelming. Using the church calendar is a helpful alternative.

The church calendar starts in Advent, signaled by the color purple, a color associated with both repentance and royalty. We prepare for the arrival (the meaning of the word "advent") of King Jesus. This time of preparation is marked by an extraordinary moment before the event, the hush before the orchestra performs, the moment before the sun rises, a time when we hold our breath. These are Advent moments, and the church has a season of holding its collective breath, so to speak, to start the liturgical year.

It is Advent, which usually comes after Thanksgiving, and not January 1 that begins the Western Christian year. The Christian year starts in rest, waiting, making room for Jesus. We remember the coming of Jesus into the world, the coming of Jesus into our life, and the return of Jesus to judge the living and the dead. We sit in figurative darkness in our spirituality just as we sit in physical darkness in this time of the year. This season of silence and waiting is a fitting time for the contemplative practices in the beauty tradition.

One of the interesting things about the church calendar is how it cuts across the secular calendar. How would you describe life and culture between Thanksgiving and Christmas? Usually, people are hurried, rushed, stressed, busy. There may be some kindness sprinkled in, but overall, it is a consumeristic hellscape in every store. For most of our neighbors, the year starts not with rest but with consumption.

The church tells time differently. In all this reordering of time, the church offers an invitation to the larger world: What kind of life do you want? You can live at rest too. You don't have to live into a fractured and rushed world. Peace is possible.

Then Christmas comes, not as a day but as a twelve-day feast. The light comes into the world, symbolized by white liturgical vestments, and for twelve days the church celebrates. The world may be exhausted by December 25, but the church is just getting started. By engaging in contemplation, analyzing our lives, and making room for Christ, we go into the world with feasting. Parties and presents are prevalent for twelve whole days. The twelfth day is called "Epiphany," and on it we commemorate the magi coming to honor the Christ child and the good news of God spreading to the gentiles. Historically, many in the church celebrated Epiphany by burning dry Christmas trees to proclaim Christ as the light of the world. If you've never burned a Christmas tree, I highly recommend it. Christians should be the best at throwing parties.

Then, until Lent, the church lives through "Ordinary Time." The liturgical color is green, which symbolizes growth. So much of our lives is lived in the ordinary moments, in which we have opportunities for normal growth. Focusing on the truth tradition during Ordinary Time would be a fitting practice.

Lent begins with Ash Wednesday, which falls anywhere from early February to early March. Ash Wednesday is a visceral reminder that we will die. Christianity, after all, is not merely about living well but is about living well in light of our death. Lent is a forty-day period (not counting Sundays) in which we follow Christ into the wilderness. As Israel was tempted for forty years to reveal what was in their hearts, so Jesus was led to the wilderness to fast and pray and be tempted by the devil to reveal what was in his heart (Matt. 4:1–10). Where Israel failed, Jesus succeeded, and his success ultimately culminates in his death. During Lent we focus on the broken aspects of our lives that need healing, looking forward to the healing that Jesus brings.

Typically, the church practices asceticism in the goodness tradition during Lent—things like fasting from certain foods or other luxuries. Remember that asceticism is not a masochistic requirement. It's not just hard for hard's sake. Giving up certain goods is a requirement for joy's sake. As Saint Augustine remarks, "How hard and painful does this appear! The Lord has required that 'whoever will come after him must deny himself.' But what he commands is neither hard nor painful when he himself helps us in such a way so that the very thing he requires may be accomplished. . . . For whatever seems hard in what is enjoined, love makes easy."[23] We all

---

23. Augustine, "Letter 243, to Laetus," in Oden and Hall, *Mark*, 106.

sacrifice for what gives us joy. I wake up early with my kids because I love them and it's a way to love my wife. You may sacrifice and work out because you want the greater good of health. We take time to read for the greater good of learning. And sometimes those things don't seem like sacrifices, because the thing we are sacrificing for is so much better than the thing sacrificed. In Jesus's case, the One who commands us to deny ourselves denies himself. The One who calls us to take up our cross helps us carry it. These practices of giving up give us more in the end.

The final days of Lent are called the Paschal Triduum. These three services—Maundy Thursday, Good Friday, and Holy Saturday—are actually one continuous service in which the church walks with Jesus through his suffering and death. Personally, these days are my favorite liturgical holidays ("holy days"). On Thursday the church leaders wash members' feet, following the example of Jesus washing the disciples' feet. Then the people remember Jesus's betrayal, and all the liturgical colors and elements are stripped from the altar. It's a tangible reminder of how the disciples, after being served by their leader, have their hopes crushed. It seems that Jesus failed. The despair and hurt I feel as I strip the altar and look at the bare church always grips me. Then, on Good Friday, there is a somber service recalling the final hours and the crucifixion of Jesus. On Holy Saturday we remember Jesus's descent to the dead and the silence of God until nightfall, when Easter tidings begin to ring.

While Lent focuses on what needs to be healed, Easter is a season that celebrates the healing. Since we are embodied beings, fasting helps me feel the longing I should have for Christ. I remember the first time I fasted during Lent. I gave up meat. When Easter morning came, my body was with my affections, longing for a more tangible reality of Christ's coming. The longing was not just in my head for what I should know; I felt it in my body. I smoked pork shoulder, grilled some meat, and feasted. And this was only the start! Easter starts a fifty-day celebration season.

One of my favorite things about the church calendar is that Easter always comes. Healing is always on the way. No matter how well, or poorly, I succeed in my fasting and prayers of Lent, Easter still comes—even with my broken promises and practices. Easter does not depend on my success in Lent. God comes with grace to save and to heal and to reconcile once again.

Fifty days after Easter, Pentecost arrives. On this day the church celebrates the coming of the Holy Spirit, the Comforter (Luke 24:49; John 14:26; 16:7–15; Acts 2:1–13). The Holy Spirit is what empowers the community to live together in love and graciousness as individual members bear the fruit of the Spirit and walk in step with the Spirit (Gal. 5:16–26).

After Pentecost, for about half of the church calendar, the church lives in Ordinary Time again. The ordinary means of grace are always present: hearing the Word preached, seeing the Word in the sacraments, singing the Word in community, engaging in practices of contemplation or asceticism. Ordinary Time is a time for ordinary growth and for living into the practices and rhythms of redemption. Maybe showing up is all you can muster some of the time. The church will pray for you. In other Ordinary Times, perhaps a deep Bible study of one book of the Bible is needed. Sometimes, Ordinary Time may feel like Advent, a season of waiting, and God may invite you into wordless silence in his presence.

So far I haven't mentioned different feast days throughout the year that celebrate martyrs and saints of the past, but those exist too.

The church calendar helps us live in time differently, remembering the story of God throughout the year. Each season helps heal our vision, which has been blurred and blinded. Each time period helps us contemplate God by focusing on a distinct diadem of his glory. As the priest Luke Bell claims, "The liturgy is about fixing our hearts where true gladness is found."[24] The yearly liturgy, as well as the weekly liturgy, helps reorder our desire.

LIVING INTO PLACE

Earlier in this chapter I mentioned Father Giles and the importance of vows of stability in the Benedictine monastic life. Stability is important for church life, and it's also important for neighborly life. In other words, stability is not merely a commitment to a holy

---

24. Bell, *Meaning of Blue*, 176.

huddle but can also be a commitment for stewarding a communal shalom.

People aren't disposable. Places aren't the same. Sure, I can make new friends, but I'll never have friends like Nick, Danny, Logan, Jack, Matt, and Ben, because they've known me the longest. They knew me in my foolish high school years. They've seen me grow. They have loved me when I felt unlovable. I've made new friends, but I can't replace my day-one homies.

Likewise, I could never have friends like Jonathon and Gary if I left Asheville, North Carolina. Our friendships are distinct. We've shared life together, cried together, worshiped together. Even if I move to a different house within the same city, I'll never have neighbors like Luis and Marianne. I can meet new neighbors, and perhaps they'll offer unique gifts. But Luis makes tacos for my family when my wife is sick. Luis introduced me to the wonder of Oaxaca, his home region in Mexico, and its signature agave plants. These are gifts that are not replaceable.

As I talk about stability, I can't promise I'll never move, but I always want to live in a place as if I'll be there forever. Doing so commits me there. Commitment also makes it hurt to leave. It should feel like I'm being ripped out of a web of connections if I leave a place, because I am. If I lived in a place and it didn't hurt to leave, then I don't think I ever cared for it or was nourished by it. If I'm not caring for a place and people, then my love for God is mental and ethereal but makes no impact on where I live. I'm not sure that's the kind of peace and healing that God is passionate about bringing to earth.

In the aftermath of the first sin, the reaction is to shift responsibility. God asks Adam, "Who told you that you were naked? Have you eaten of the tree of which I commanded you not to eat?" (Gen. 3:11). Adam points his finger in blame: "The woman whom you gave to be with me, she gave me fruit of the tree, and I ate" (v. 12). When Cain kills Abel and God comes looking, Cain asks, "Am I my brother's keeper?" (4:9). The implied answer to this rhetorical question is no, but the real answer is yes. Yes! You are your brother's keeper. When Christ comes, he comes bearing the guilt as his brother's keeper. He takes responsibility. Spiritual formation is misguided and distorted if you don't bind yourself to a connected community, which includes the land and all living creatures.

We are placed beings. We are taken from the land, and we feed on the land. We cannot avoid the truth that "our land passes in and out of our bodies just as our bodies pass in and out of our land" and that all the living "are part of one another, and so cannot possibly flourish alone."[25] We are in a web of existence that includes not only the church and our neighbors but also the very dirt we live on. Creation care is therefore spiritual formation. Caring for the land is stewarding God's gifts to us. Every created thing is loved by God. But we will not love what we do not know. As Wendell Berry says, "To see and respect what is there is the first duty of stewardship."[26] Perhaps the reason we don't care much about the maintenance of what we've been given is that our hands seldom touch the land. We drive on pavement and walk on cement. Part of the creation mandate of Genesis 1 is ecological care as an act of dominion—not dominance but watchfulness.

On the subject of living into place, the theologian Norman Wirzba proposes, "If you want to be with God, don't look up and away to some destination far beyond the blue. Look down and around, because that is where God is at work and where God wants to be. God does not ever flee from his creatures."[27] God meets his creatures where they are. God is not around the next bend, at the next big event. God is here, among us, desiring to meet us. Adam is taken from the *adamah*, the ground. Humans come from humus. God inspires the dirt to create humanity. We're called to toil and serve the dirt we came from. We're called to nourish the places that have nourished us. Often, however, we forsake the dirt and fail to live with the land. We deteriorate our genesis.

In an interview with nature writer Barry Lopez, Fred Bahnson asked about Lopez's time in the 1970s and 1980s among the Inuit population in the Arctic. Lopez asked what adjective these indigenous communities would use to describe white North American culture. The word he heard again and again was "lonely." "They see us as

25. Berry, *Unsettling of America*, 22.
26. Berry, "Native Grasses and What They Mean," 53.
27. Wirzba, *Agrarian Spirit*, 5.

deeply lonely people," Barry told Fred, "and one of the reasons we're lonely is that we've cut ourselves off from the nonhuman world and have called this 'progress.'"[28] Maturity in Christ is not escape but presence.

Early in my spiritual life, I knew to care about the land, but I did not care to know about the land. And those few swapped words make a world of difference. The modern world encourages us to try to live as disembodied entities, disconnected from both time and place. We may feel like technology gives us access to every place, but every place is no place. Likewise, every time is no time. Because I buy my food in a package at the grocery store, I am disconnected from the earth and its corresponding seasons, rhythms, and cycles. I don't know the effects of extended drought or what season certain vegetables grow in. I go to the supermarket, and every season is no season.

"People *exploit* what they have merely concluded to be of value, but they *defend* what they love," Berry argues in an essay. "And to defend what we love we need a particularizing language, for we love what we particularly know."[29] An agrarian mindset invites us to nourish life in holistic ways: creating vitality of land, creatures, and people together. It invites us to care for and to love our place and our neighbors.

CONCLUSION

I grew up in Cleveland, Ohio. When I was young, I lamented my place. I always wanted to leave Cleveland. I'd visit "cool" places like Chicago and see that they had so much more . . . stuff: buildings, restaurants, parks, culture. Even if both Cleveland and Chicago tended to be cold and bitter, with long winters and gray, dreary skies, cities like Chicago seemed hip. Cleveland was boring.

When I left Cleveland for "cooler" places, I realized how much I loved Cleveland. I didn't know how much it had formed me until I was gone. Place is funny like that. We don't appreciate things until we lose them. Now that I've left, I have a new appreciation for Cleveland.

28. Bahnson, "Unbroken Grace."
29. Berry, *Life Is a Miracle*, 41.

I can't say I dream of returning, but there's a longing and love I feel for it. It's not the best city in the world, but it is my city. I grew to care for it, and it hurt to leave.

It should always hurt to leave. There are reasons for moving on. I live in Asheville now (which is one of those cool places—I lucked out). But there will never be a place like Cleveland in my life. It loved me into being. It formed how I view the world (and determined the blessed sports team I love). The goal of the Christian life is to love our place before we leave it, to grow affection for it, to connect to God, land, and place where we are. Where we are is where God wants to meet us.

✳ 12 ✳

DIETRICH BONHOEFFER

NEIGHBOR LOVE AND LIFE TOGETHER

I was first introduced to the life and thought of Dietrich Bonhoeffer in a seminar at Gordon College on the North Shore of Boston. It was an upperclassmen seminar, full of group discussions and presentations. The class was held in a rotunda overlooking Coy Pond, an idyllic setting in which to start my research into a man who plotted to kill Hitler and was later executed.

After I finished the course, Bonhoeffer sat dormant in my mind until I was meeting with my friends Bethany and Steven to talk about starting an intentional community where we would farm, care for the poor, and live together. This vision of connectedness and wholeness compelled me—caring for the land and caring for the least of these.

One day, Steven sent out an email that began with a quote from Dietrich Bonhoeffer's *Life Together*, a book I had read during that course at Gordon College. Bonhoeffer is worth quoting at length:

> Just at this point Christian brotherhood is threatened most often at the very start by the greatest danger of all, the danger of being poisoned at its root, the danger of confusing Christian brotherhood with some wishful idea of religious fellowship, of confounding the natural

desire of the devout heart for community with the spiritual reality of Christian brotherhood. In Christian brotherhood everything depends upon its being clear right from the beginning, first, that Christian brotherhood is not an ideal, but a divine reality. Second, that Christian brotherhood is a spiritual and not a psychic reality.

Innumerable times a whole Christian community has broken down because it has sprung from a wish dream. The serious Christian, set down for the first time in a Christian community is likely to bring with him a very definite idea of what Christian life together should be and to try to realize it. But God's grace speedily shatters such dreams. Just as surely as God desires to lead us to a knowledge of genuine Christian fellowship, so surely must we be overwhelmed by a great disillusionment with others, with Christians in general, and, if we are fortunate, with ourselves. . . .

He who loves his dream of a community more than the Christian community itself becomes a destroyer of the latter, even though his personal intentions may be ever so honest and earnest and sacrificial.[1]

Idealism, what Bonhoeffer calls a wish dream, destroys the reality of Christian community. Bonhoeffer is not against an ideal church or the desire for the purity of the church. But if wanting a picture-perfect community makes you forsake the church, then your idealism is useless. You're rejecting Christ, who is already there. He goes on to say that God hates the visionary dreamer.

Bonhoeffer gave his life to the work of the church and to strengthening church communities. His dissertation was titled *Sanctorum Communio*, or "The Communion of Saints." Later, when pressing political issues were ripe in Germany, he set out to write a field guide called *Life Together* for a seminary he helped start. The seminary lasted a little over two years before it was shut down by Nazi officials.

In a 1933 essay entitled "What Is the Church?" Bonhoeffer offers his definition of the church:

It is an institution that is not a good model of organization, not very influential, not very impressive, in need of improvement in the extreme. However, church is a ministry from God, a ministry of proclamation, the message of the living God. From it come commission and

1. Bonhoeffer, *Life Together*, 26–27.

commandment; in it arise eternal ties; in it heaven and hell clash; in it the judgment on earth takes place. Because church is the living Christ and his judgment. The preached and preaching Christ, proclaimer and proclamation, ministry and word. Church is the awakening of the world through a miracle, through the presence of the life-creating God calling from death into life.[2]

Bonhoeffer was aware of the church's flaws, but he was more aware of the miracle of Christ in community. Elsewhere, he insists, "It is grace, nothing but grace, that we are allowed to live in community with Christian brethren."[3] Sure, church is imperfect, but it is also the concrete community that responds to Christ's speaking. Therefore, the church is grace all the way through.

At the center of many churches is a crucifix, on which Jesus Christ hangs dead. We all come to church gathered around a humiliated Savior. Rather than hope for a wish dream, Bonhoeffer says, join the embarrassment. Embrace the discomfort. Work where God has you, because Christ resides in that community of the church.[4] Don't go looking elsewhere.

The intriguing part about Bonhoeffer's commitment to the church is that he had every reason to become embittered, frustrated, and critical. If anyone had a reason to abandon the institution of the church, it was Dietrich Bonhoeffer. The modern American church is imperfect, but we haven't pledged allegiance to the Führer as our supreme ruler. In Bonhoeffer's day the German church passed a resolution to remove any clergy and leaders from office if they were of Jewish descent. This travesty led to the crafting of the Barmen Declaration, which separated the Confessing Church from the Lutheran Church in Germany. Rather than abandon the church, Bonhoeffer sought to renew and build up the church. He knew the church enough to love it, because he knew that was where Christ was. In the words of novelist and essayist Marilynne Robinson, "In

2. Bonhoeffer, *Berlin: 1932–1933*, 263.
3. Bonhoeffer, *Life Together*, 20.
4. "The whole point of this distinction between the work of Christ and that of the Spirit is that it allows Bonhoeffer to maintain that the church really is a reality of revelation, but that it is so in a way that (from our human and sinful standpoint) is never directly available to us" (Mawson, *Christ Existing as Community*, 130).

Bonhoeffer's understanding, the otherness of God is precisely this boundless compassion."[5] Bonhoeffer displayed this "boundless compassion" to fellow church members and to his neighbors, even those who needed to be corrected.

Bonhoeffer is a complex figure.[6] There are as many "takes" on Bonhoeffer as there are writers. Everyone wants to use Bonhoeffer for their own theory or tradition—liberal theologians say he was a liberal, evangelicals say he was evangelical, pacifists say he was a pacifist, and just-war theorists say his plotting to kill Hitler indicates a change of mind. In writing this chapter, I am weary of using Bonhoeffer to make a point about church and community. Some may argue he was against the church, as he spoke of "religionless Christianity";[7] the institution of the church is certainly part of religion. Bonhoeffer is a complex figure because he was a complex thinker. He cannot be stereotyped or condensed or neatly packaged. So, as best we can, we must take Bonhoeffer as he presents himself rather than fashion him in our own image.

BONHOEFFER'S BACKGROUND

Born into a family of seven children in 1906, Bonhoeffer was raised in an academic and comfortable environment. Many of his siblings would become coconspirators in a plot to overthrow Hitler. His father was a well-known physician and was surprised when Bonhoeffer decided that he wanted to be a pastor and theologian. Two ideas are essential to understanding Bonhoeffer, according to Robinson: "first, that the sacred can be inferred from the world in the experience of goodness, beauty, and love; and second, that these things, and, more generally, the immanence of God are a real presence, not a symbol or a foreshadowing. They are fulfillment as well as promise, like the sacrament, or the church."[8] Bonhoeffer encountered God not only

5. Robinson, *Death of Adam*, 110.
6. See Haynes, *Bonhoeffer Phenomenon*.
7. For Bonhoeffer, religionless Christianity was getting to the core of Christianity, as he saw holy orders and the sacraments being defiled in support of Hitler. He was seeing Christians who took on the name of Christ and yet committed atrocities.
8. Robinson, *Death of Adam*, 122.

through ideas but among creatures. He was able to see divine realities in ordinary or dark circumstances.

At twenty-two years old, he earned his doctorate in Berlin before traveling to New York. In 1930 Bonhoeffer visited Abyssinian Baptist Church in Harlem, a historically African American and impoverished neighborhood, while studying and lecturing at Union Theological Seminary. The experience at this church was formative for young Bonhoeffer. He began to see the church from the perspective of the disenfranchised and downcast rather than the strong and powerful. He committed to this urban church and began to teach Sunday school. These experiences made a profound difference in his vision of the church. In *Life Together* he writes, "The exclusion of the weak and insignificant, the seemingly useless people, from a Christian community may actually be the exclusion of Christ; in the poor brother Christ is knocking at the door. We must, therefore, be very careful at this point."[9] In Harlem he also learned of Black spirituals, and he would later take back to Germany a record collection that he played at his seminary at Finkenwalde. It's a staggering idea that a group of German intellectuals and pastors suffering under the weight of Nazi oppression were listening to sources of hope and renewal from Black Americans like Mahalia Jackson.

Seeing the minority church in America gave Bonhoeffer a vision for the church in Germany. For example, when Nazi Germany began euthanizing the incurably sick, Bonhoeffer had to speak up for the weak and insignificant. In an important and oft-quoted work called "The Church and the Jewish Question," Bonhoeffer outlines his political theology. How should the church relate to the government? First, the church questions the legitimacy of the state's action. The church reminds the government that it has a responsibility. It speaks prophetically for the sake of those who are overlooked or unseen. Second, the church serves the victims of the state. Bonhoeffer writes, "The church has an unconditional obligation toward the victims of any societal order, even if they do not belong to the Christian community."[10] Not only is the church to speak prophetically to the powers that be, but Christians are to be prophets of action, binding up the wounds of

9. Bonhoeffer, *Life Together*, 38.
10. Bonhoeffer, "The Church and the Jewish Question," 226.

victims. As described in the previous chapter, the church is called to be not a holy huddle but a communal shalom. The church must care for those whom the state ignores or persecutes. We are in a web of existence, after all. Lastly, and perhaps most well known, the church is not only to speak out and help the victims of the state but is also, if necessary, to put itself in harm's way. The illustration Bonhoeffer uses is a car or bike running over victims. At a certain point, the church has to "fall into the spokes"; that is, Christians must sacrificially lay down their lives to stop the car or bike from continuing. The church must give up all privilege in speaking out for the voiceless. Bonhoeffer writes, "Real secularity consists in the church's being able to renounce all privileges and all its property but never Christ's Word and the forgiveness of sins. With Christ and the forgiveness of sins to fall back on, the church is free to give up everything else."[11] In other words, there are a few chosen elements of the church that we should never abandon without abandoning Christ—namely, Christ's word and forgiveness of sins. In most everything else, we should be fairly adaptable.

In the end, Bonhoeffer gave everything up. He saw the German church as being at the final step of engagement with the political authorities. He cared for victims of injustice. He spoke prophetically. After seeing the continued suffering and victimization that the government caused, he fell into the spokes. He could not stand idly by. He advocated for the victims of the state and was arrested for his part in a plot to assassinate Hitler. This act of love cost Bonhoeffer his life.

Bonhoeffer was himself compelled into action by his understanding of his own identity in the world. He realized that the Jewish question was the church's question. There is a cosmic belonging between people in place. As Laura Fabrycky documents in her memoir on volunteering at the Bonhoeffer house, "The difference wasn't in their knowing the right thing to do. What mattered was how they understood who they were (identity) in relationship to others (belonging). How they imagined their belonging to others is what determined how they behaved."[12] Dietrich Bonhoeffer imagined himself as belonging to the least of these, and that reality determined how he behaved and how he

---

11. Bonhoeffer, *Testament to Freedom*, 92.
12. Fabrycky, *Keys to Bonhoeffer's Haus*, 85.

suggested the church should function. He was able to see God among people and creatures. He saw the web of connection. Where there were two or three Christians gathered, Jesus was there with them (Matt. 18:20). When we serve "the least of these" (25:40), Jesus is among them. With Jesus, Bonhoeffer sees God through personal encounters with embodied individuals. Drawing on this logic, Michael Mawson notes, "It is only through this concrete human other that God places the human person into a situation of ethical decision and obligation."[13]

CHRIST EXISTING AS COMMUNITY

In *From Isolation to Community*, Myles Werntz uses Dietrich Bonhoeffer as a guide for community building and church habits, not because Bonhoeffer is a practical guru but because he offers a "theological therapy."[14] I like the phrase, and I think it is fitting. Bonhoeffer does not show us the three steps to a better church or small-group program. Rather, he invites us to consider what the church is and how we should go about seeking healing and wholeness in an isolated and fragmented world. He helps us imagine the church as a different place.

There are two essential insights from Bonhoeffer on Christianity and the church: Christianity must be social, and Christianity is not merely social.[15] Being social and being in Christ are two sides of a single coin.

First, Christianity is inherently social. The pursuit of Christ always happens in community. Spiritual formation occurs with others. Theology never happens in isolation. When we take on the trinitarian name in baptism, this act happens *to* us. We don't baptize ourselves; we need someone else. Jesus is not merely accepted into our hearts; he is the cornerstone of a new belonging that results in community.[16] Bonhoeffer implores the Christian, "But if we have been

13. Mawson, *Christ Existing as Community*, 64.
14. Werntz, *From Isolation to Community*, 9.
15. This insight is in Werntz, *From Isolation to Community*, which summarizes two of Bonhoeffer's lesser-known works, *Act and Being* and *Sanctorum Communio*.
16. Even by himself, Bonhoeffer recognizes the undeniable reality of communion. "The prisoner, the sick person, the Christian living in the diaspora recognizes in the nearness of a fellow Christian a physical sign of the gracious presence of the triune God. They receive each other's blessings as the blessings of the Lord Jesus Christ" (Bonhoeffer, *Life Together*, 18).

elected and accepted with the whole church in Jesus Christ before we could know it or want it, then we also belong to Christ in eternity with one another. We who live here in community with Christ will one day be with Christ in eternal community."[17] The foundation of being in Christ is the foundation of community. We don't have one without the other.

Having spent much of my adult life in church leadership, I've seen many people come and go from church. Some people leave for good reasons, others for shallow ones, but when people choose to go, they're typically not looking for feedback. Their decision is already made.

As people have left our church, one of the most frustrating comments has been "But you guys are still my main community." These people leave our church for another one, never making deep friendships with their new church community. They imagine they can get Christ better somewhere else, since they like the preaching or music or ministry programs better there, while getting community over here, where they have no commitment. In so doing they implicitly sever Christ from community, playing into modern divisions and fragmentations. In reality, Christ and community are one.

In Bonhoeffer's understanding, Christ always exists as community. We cannot separate those two things. The ethic of Jesus is embodied in community. In the church we are united by a work of God—not affinities or nationalities or skin color or age or preference. In the editorial introduction of *Life Together*, the writers propose, "The Christ of *Life Together* is the binding force of that community in its 'togetherness,' gracing Christians to go beyond the superficial, often self-centered, relationships of their everyday associations toward a more intimate sense of what it means to be Christ to others, to love others as Christ has loved them."[18] We're bound in community by Christ's call, not by whom we like or whom we prefer to be with. This community may include our natural enemies, and there is "no offering which a lover would bring to a beloved" that "can be too great for our enemies."[19] The church creates a community open to all who respond to the call of Christ—including not just those we

17. Bonhoeffer, *Life Together*, 33.
18. Introduction to *Life Together*, *Prayerbook of the Bible*, 8.
19. Bonhoeffer, *Discipleship*, 139.

don't prefer but even our very enemies. Christ exists in community, so Christianity is always social.

Second, Christianity is not merely social. The other side of Bonhoeffer's legacy is his idea that community exists in Christ. Sometimes people think of the church merely as a social gathering, a place to build fulfilling relationships. The church functions as a social club rather than a place where people encounter Christ. Thus, when change happens in the community, people leave.

On one level, being in Christ means that the church should not be organized according to age or interests or status. On a deeper level, Christ existing as community means that even family relationships—those between husband and wife, children and parents, and so on—are mediated by Christ. Every relationship has Christ as its core. As Bonhoeffer advocates, "Spiritual love, however, comes from Jesus Christ; it serves him alone. It knows that it has no direct access to other persons. Christ stands between me and others."[20] We love others in Christ and not as we prefer them. By seeing Christ in others, we enable ourselves to love them for who they are and not who we wish they would be.

CONCLUSION

Bonhoeffer didn't seek community for community's sake. He didn't turn community into the church's ultimate end, into an idol of sorts. But as I've argued, he invited the church to pursue truth, goodness, and beauty, and community emerged from the pursuit. Community was the deepening effect of Bonhoeffer's broad spiritual direction.

He had a deep commitment to the truth of the Scriptures. When Bonhoeffer's friend and correspondent was asked about the spiritual practices at Finkenwalde, he replied, "Why do I meditate? Because I am a Christian, and because therefore every day is a day lost for me in which I have not penetrated deeper into the understanding of the Word of God."[21] The Bible was central to forming a community in Christ's name.

20. Bonhoeffer, *Life Together*, 43.
21. Bosanquet, *Life and Death of Dietrich Bonhoeffer*, 157.

Bonhoeffer also developed a rule of life, which he outlined in *Life Together*. The community had rhythms and habits of prayer, work, and study. They wanted to be good and Christlike, to care for and love "the least of these." To be a certain kind of people, they needed the habits that formed virtue. It wasn't legalistic, but it was formative.

Lastly, Bonhoeffer described his community as a "new monasticism."[22] The linking of the centrality of Scripture with the rhythms of a monastic life served the purpose of purging the self and uniting people with each other and with God. Bonhoeffer desired to develop a community that was intentional about seeking the face of God, because from encounter flows transformation. He sought beauty in the face of Christ.

All of these transcendentals were wrapped in community. Even the silence of solitary prayer connected them to the company of heaven and earth.[23] By praying in solitude, we become more aware that our prayers are wrapped around the community of saints.

From his prison cell, Bonhoeffer wrote his old friend Eberhard Bethge about holding the "cantus firmus," a strong melody amid a polyphony of music.

> Where the cantus firmus is clear and plain, the counterpoint can be developed to its limits. . . . Have a good clear cantus firmus; that is the only way to a full and perfect sound, when the counterpoint has a firm support and can't come adrift or get out of tune, while remaining a distinct whole in its own right. Only a polyphony of this kind can give life a wholeness and at the same time assure us that nothing calamitous can happen as long as the cantus firmus is kept going.[24]

In *Life Together* he was attempting to find the fullness of the cantus firmus amid life's tragedies and dirges. He sang the tune no matter what sound was going on around him.

The life of Dietrich Bonhoeffer was extinguished on April 9, 1945, at the Flossenbürg concentration camp. One British prisoner said that in his last days Bonhoeffer "always seemed to diffuse an atmosphere

---

22. Bonhoeffer, *Testament to Freedom*, 424.
23. Bosanquet, *Life and Death of Dietrich Bonhoeffer*, 157–59.
24. Bonhoeffer, *Letters and Papers from Prison*, 303.

of happiness, of joy in every smallest event in life, and a deep grati-tude for the mere fact that he was alive."[25] He died alone, yet he was surrounded and upheld by the community of the faithful, and the faithful saints of all ages welcomed him home.

PRACTICES

CHURCH COMMITMENT

Whether our church invites us to commit through the ritual of confirmation or official membership or simply regular attendance, we all need to belong to a place. We need to know and be known by others. Christ calls us into his church, which is embodied in local, physical locations. You're called to "obey your leaders and submit to them" (Heb. 13:17). It's no light or easy decision; we all should get to know a local church and its leaders and see if they are worthy of that obedience. Then jump in and stay.

ACCOUNTABILITY

We need other people. One of the primary means of growth is other people. Proverbs says, "Iron sharpens iron, and one man sharp-ens another" (Prov. 27:17). By consistently meeting, confessing sin, and pursuing Christ in relationship, close friends can build relation-ships that mirror those between siblings. No one will be best friends with everyone, but everyone ought to have a few trusted friends whom they can tell anything to and who have permission to call them out. There is also something healing about confessing sins with a trusted friend rather than vaguely thinking about sin before God. These verbal acts can be the beginning of transformation. Spiritual friends come to us as gifts that keep us accountable.

HOSPITALITY

When hospitality is mentioned in the New Testament, it is always connected with love (Rom. 12:9–13; Heb. 13:1–2; 1 Pet. 4:8–9). The

25. Introduction to *Life Together*, 13.

call to hospitality (literally "the love of strangers") is the call to connect with others who may have no relational connections, who may be overlooked or overseen. The practice of table fellowship, or sharing a meal, is a way to welcome the stranger and turn them into the family of God. It's a practical way to love your neighbor and connect them to community.

ENCOURAGEMENT

We live in a society void of encouragement. People are starving for positive feedback and appreciation. One of the practices for building community and cultivating gratitude is writing notes (handwritten, preferably) to those in your life who have been an encouragement. This practice builds up others and helps you be more grateful and more awake to the ways God uses other people in your life.

RESOURCES

Berry, Wendell. *Jayber Crow*. Berkeley: Counterpoint, 2000.

Pohl, Christine D. *Living into Community: Cultivating Practices That Sustain Us*. Grand Rapids: Eerdmans, 2012.

Thurman, Howard. *Jesus and the Disinherited*. Boston: Beacon, 1993.

Wirzba, Norman. *Agrarian Spirit: Cultivating Faith, Community, and the Land*. Notre Dame, IN: University of Notre Dame Press, 2022.

Conclusion

WHOLE PERSONS AND HOLY PERSONS

> One of the lasting legacies of the early church, then, is the recognition that doctrine, prayer, and ethics don't exist in tidy separate compartments: each one shapes the others. And in the church in any age, we should not be surprised if we become lazy about our doctrine at a time when we are less clear about our priorities as a community, or if we become less passionate about service, forgiveness, and peace when we have stopped thinking clearly about the true and eternal character of God.
>
> —Rowan Williams, *The Two Ways*

In the movie *Talladega Nights*, Will Ferrell plays a race car driver named Ricky Bobby. One day, when he is a child, his absentee father shows up at Ricky's classroom for Career Day. Shocked after not seeing his father for eight years, Ricky Bobby is excited to hear from his dad, who is a semi-professional race car driver and an amateur tattoo artist.

Ricky's dad gets kicked out of class for encouraging kids not to listen to their "know-it-all teacher" and a few other controversial remarks. After being forcibly removed, he peels out of the parking lot and shouts to his son, "Always remember, Ricky: if you ain't first, you're last."

Ricky Bobby goes on to become a famous race car driver. But after a tragic accident, he has trouble going fast again. At his low point, Ricky's dad comes back in the picture, and Ricky confesses that he has achieved all his fame because of those parting words from his dad. His dad admits he was high on drugs when he said that, because it doesn't make any sense at all. "You can be second, third, fourth. Hell, you can even be fifth."

Hurt, Ricky declares, "I've lived my whole life by that phrase."

THE SEARCH FOR REST

I began this book by describing my own unrest. As Ronald Rolheiser says, spirituality is what we do with our unrest.[1] We try to place our rest in different external pursuits. In the phrase of Saint Augustine, our hearts are made for God, and we won't rest until we rest in him.[2] I can say to Augustine something very similar to what Ricky Bobby says to his father: I understand my whole life by that phrase. I take comfort in the knowledge that others have found that phrase to be true to reality.

The search for rest is the human predicament. In the pursuits of truth, goodness, beauty, and community, we are on a quest for rest. All of us desire to be known and loved by God and to know and love others in return. The end of rest is a life of eternal love.

When God saves us, he doesn't give us a laundry list of faults and sins we must conquer. He doesn't expose all that we don't know. That would be cruel and overwhelming. Can you imagine? Rather, he graciously reveals one step and one sin at a time, slowly refining us—sometimes slower than we wish. In my own life, it seems the closer I get to God, the more sin is revealed. Unrest is part of the Christian life. We're pilgrims journeying to the homeland, but the homeland is yet to come. Our citizenship is in heaven, from which the Savior will come (Phil. 3:20). If the end of rest is eternal love, then it's no surprise we're not there yet.

In the meantime, our unrest is channeled into growth. We become broad and deep people as we increase in truth, goodness, beauty, and community. Saint Gregory of Nyssa advises, "Let no one be grieved if he sees in his nature a penchant for change. Changing in everything for the better, let him exchange 'glory for glory' [2 Cor. 3:18], becoming greater through daily increase, ever perfecting himself. . . . For this

1. Rolheiser, *Holy Longing*, 5.
2. Augustine, *Confessions* 1.1.1.

is truly perfection: never to stop growing towards what is better and never placing any limit on perfection."[3] The Transcendent One can never be exhausted. He's always inviting us into deeper life with him.

WHERE TO START?

I began this book with the truth tradition because it is the foundation of spirituality. But there are some who would argue that we ought to begin in beauty, because that's how we start every pursuit. We aren't convinced by all the reasons Jesus is the Son of God. Rather, we experience his beauty, and we're compelled to follow him. Answers are sought as a result of encounter. Philosopher Peter Kreeft believes that "beauty is the ambassador for truth and goodness; we fall in love with the beauty of a theology or of a morality first—and the same is true of a religion."[4] We are compelled and drawn into Christ, and then we work out our questions and virtue in the aftermath of that initial attraction. Theologian David Bentley Hart says the whole of our existence is poetic, founded in beauty. Hart argues,

> The truth of being is "poetic" before it is "rational" (indeed, it is rational precisely because of its supreme poetic coherence and richness of detail), and this cannot be known truly if this order is reversed. Beauty is the beginning and end of all true knowledge: really to know, one must first love, and having known, one must finally delight; only this "corresponds" to the Trinitarian love and delight that creates.[5]

Beauty is the means and end of life with God. Knowing the Bible, practicing virtue, and living in community are all directed to the end of beauty: seeing God in his fullness. To make any other pursuit an end is idolatry. All things must be subordinate to the beauty of God. Seeing God is life in heaven.

Hans Urs von Balthasar was a twentieth-century theologian known for his work on theological aesthetics and beauty. Writing in a time of stale and dry academic theology, von Balthasar thought it was a

3. Gregory of Nyssa, *On Perfection*, 121–22.
4. Kreeft, "Beauty Is the First Thing We Notice and Love."
5. Hart, "Offering of Names," 26–27.

travesty to make as rich and beautiful a subject as God dry and boring. Summarizing von Balthasar's work, John W. de Gruchy writes, "Truth without goodness and beauty degenerates into dogmatism, and lacks the power to attract and convince; goodness without truth is superficial, and without beauty—that is without graced form— degenerates into moralism. Alternatively, we could say that truth and goodness without beauty lack power to convince and therefore to save."[6] Along the same lines, Jennifer Allen Craft adds,

> Balthasar's theological aesthetics are relevant here in terms of Christian mission as he demonstrates the ways in which the power of beauty and love can bring forth both ethical action (goodness) and true contemplation of the form of God (truth), the ancient transcendental formulation of beauty, goodness, and truth suggesting something of this microcosmic moving out, the particular moment of Beauty apprehended in form, which motivates both ethical action and knowledge of God.[7]

As counterintuitive as it sounds, the best way to pursue spiritual formation may be to start with beauty: beauty that leads to the gospel, contemplation that leads to truth, purging that leads to union.

While it may be interesting to think about where spirituality begins, the important thing is to start somewhere. I'm indifferent as to which stream people choose as long as they start and realize that the work of formation needs to be holistic. Growth shouldn't be confined to one transcendental, or we will be malformed—as with someone who goes to the gym and only does bicep exercises. We may be prone to flex a certain muscle, so to speak, but we need a whole routine. We need all the transcendentals if we are to develop into the image of the Transcendent One.

However, God has wired us each differently, and as we discover our true selves in the presence of God, we may not look very well-rounded to those around us. All the exemplars we've seen are extreme and radical in the best sense. The work of formation is one of wholeness but not a clean well-roundedness—at least not by outward appearance. Dorothy Day was fully formed, but I'm not sure we would describe

6. De Gruchy, *Christianity, Art and Transformation*, 107.
7. Craft, *Placemaking and the Arts*, 147.

her as well-rounded. She was a love warrior for the poor and homeless. Augustine was righteously misshapen as an intellectual giant. Teresa of Ávila did not fit in as she intimately encountered Jesus. Dietrich Bonhoeffer was a radical for justice and community.

Likewise, we may be extreme. Perhaps we ought to be. And if we are, we're in good company. The work of maturity is to become a whole, holy fool. As Thérèse of Lisieux puts it, "I have no other desire than to love Jesus even unto folly."[8] Love drives us to foolishness for Christ.

HOLISTIC HOLY FOOLS

In the Eastern tradition of Christianity, especially in Russia, there is a legacy of certain people being labeled "holy fools." These are people who look foolish to the world in their pursuit of Christ. They live in weird places or eat weird things. They don't fit in. They're loony.

Holy folly has a rich biblical tradition too. David dances before the Lord in a manner that is too undignified for his wife, Michal, but he is content to be abased before her eyes in worshiping God (2 Sam. 6:20–23). Isaiah walks around Assyria naked and barefoot (Isa. 20:2). Ezekiel bakes a cake on burning dung as an object lesson for Jerusalem (Ezek. 4:12). John the Baptist preaches in the wilderness, wearing a garment of camel hair and eating honey and locusts (Matt. 3:1–4). Jesus thanks God for hiding things from the wise and revealing them to little children (Matt. 11:25). When the Holy Spirit falls on the early church on Pentecost, the people think they are drunk (Acts 2:13). Perhaps most clearly, the apostle Paul writes, "We are fools for Christ's sake" (1 Cor. 4:10). Wisdom and strength are reoriented in Christ (1 Cor. 1:18–31). Indeed, being misunderstood as fools seems to be part of the Christian witness.

John Saward describes nine different elements of holy folly, and for the sake of this discussion, I'll highlight three.[9] The first is Christocentricity: "The inspiration of all their actions is identity with Christ crucified, participation in the Lord's poverty, mockery, humiliation,

---

8. Thérèse of Lisieux, *Letters*, as quoted in Saward, *Perfect Fools*, 211.
9. Saward, *Perfect Fools*, 25–28.

nakedness, and self-emptying."[10] Holy fools identify with the weak, the homeless, the dependent, because they are following the life of Christ. If "Christian" means "little Christ," then they take that identifier seriously. The foolish love of God turns us into foolish lovers of God. If we take spiritual formation seriously, we may look strange by the world's values and standards.

Second, holy folly is eschatological. Holy fools see the conflict between what the present world values and what the kingdom of God values. There's an antithesis between this world and the world to come. Holy fools don't mind looking odd when they live by the logic of a different system. Wendell Berry has written a poem called "Manifesto: The Mad Farmer Liberation Front." In the poem, Berry encourages us to do things that don't compute: love the Lord, give to the poor, work for nothing, plant sequoias, work for a future even if it's a future you won't see this side of the resurrection. Holy folly operates with a similar value system. It won't compute by the world's logic.

Third, one of the most common motifs of holy fools is pilgrimage. They tend to be nomads. They're committed to the church and are recognized by the church, but they exhibit some restless tension. Holy fools don't divide themselves from the church, but they strengthen the church through challenge or from the margins.

Holy fools invite us to unlearn self-importance and to learn the way of simple, humble, obscure obedience. Spiritual formation is about becoming not an intellectual genius but a spiritual infant. Holy fools are holy and whole but have some rough edges. There is no cookie-cutter spirituality. Based on how God wired you, maybe there's a way for you to love Jesus unto foolishness.

So, friends, I invite you into a full formation by a theological life, a virtuous life, a beautiful life, and a connected life. Pursue Christ fully and deeply. And don't forget to be a fool.

Where there is wholeness, there is holiness. Where there is holiness, there is rest.

May your search for rest find its satisfaction in the love and presence of God.

---

10. Saward, *Perfect Fools*, 25.

Acknowledgments

Like most good things, this book was a group project. Sometimes, when I'm in a group project, I feel like I'm the only one doing anything. In this group project, I felt the group constantly holding my dead weight and carrying me to the finish line. I can't do most things by myself (try as I might), but as I reflect on this book coming together, I can't help but be especially grateful for the help I received. There are so many on whom I've depended.

I wouldn't have been able to write this book without the pastoral care I've received in my life. Thank you to Matt Koons, Jason Spodnik, Jim Hibschman, Drew Carroll, Nathan Loudin, and Gary Ball. You have all traveled with me during lows and highs. You've seen me at my worst, and you know me well enough to know when I'm faking it. I am indebted to you because of your care, teaching, love, and shepherding. If I have picked up any virtues, it is thanks to you.

When I was in seminary, Dr. Russell Moore was one of my favorite professors. We weren't particularly close, but I always admired his wisdom, grace, and personal kindness. Over the years, many of the people I looked up to as models of conviction have seemed to change convictions. It was all disorienting to me. Was I changing? Were they? Probably a little bit of both. But Dr. Moore seemed to be saying the same things with the same signature convictional kindness. He was a model of a long obedience in the same direction. He was someone

I wanted to be like. And so I couldn't be more pleased that he agreed to write the foreword. Thank you, Dr. Moore. You have encouraged me to "be good" by being Christlike—no matter the cost.

I wouldn't have been able to publish this book without the help of some acquaintances who barely knew me and owed me nothing. I am astounded by your kindness. Thank you, first, to my acquisitions editor, Bob Hosack, who believed in the project enough to help me develop and refine it. Thank you to Tim West and the editorial team at Baker Academic. Your close reading and helpful suggestions made this book much better. Thank you also to Jonathon Dodson, David Swanson, Galen Jones, Evan Howard, Jeff Tabone, and Amy Oxendale-Imig, who all wrote letters of recommendation. I have never even met many of these folks. Your kindness was undeserved and thus heightens my gratitude further. I can't repay you, but I hope I can pass on your graciousness to others.

This book would be much worse if it weren't for the help of some friends and colleagues who offered their assistance. Sam Guthrie, Anthony Rodriguez, Colby Truesdale, and Elizabeth Juckett: thanks for making me look less like an imbecile. For any semblance of understanding or helpfulness that comes with the book, I credit this group. For any errors that remain, I take full responsibility.

Thank you also to my employers, Montreat College and Redeemer Anglican Church. To my students: you have made me a better teacher and a better person. These students took my courses the first few times I ever taught them. I told them that these courses would be the worst ones I would ever teach. We suffered through them together, hopefully with moments of joy and laughter. My colleagues—especially my fellow basement dwellers—have been constant sources of encouragement and connection.

Redeemer Anglican Church: Thank you. It's a joy to serve you. Many pieces of this book were first tested during teachings or sermons. Like any church, we are a mess. But like few churches, you have consistently shown up and loved one another and my family. I love going to church and being together.

Finally, to Lauren, my wife: "Many women have done excellently, but you surpass them all" (Prov. 31:29). There's no one else I'd rather be with. I still choose you.

In many ways my life is a collection of gifts, of undeserved favors, of grace. It is by grace that I live and move and have my being. To all who have contributed to my life, thank you. You have shaped me and, by shaping me, have shaped this book.

Alex Sosler
Epiphany 2023

Bibliography

"Aftermath." *The Rise and Fall of Mars Hill* (podcast), December 4, 2021, https://podcasts.apple.com/us/podcast/the-rise-and-fall-of-mars-hill/id1569401963.

Allison, C. FitzSimons. *The Cruelty of Heresy: An Affirmation of Christian Orthodoxy*. New York: Morehouse, 1994.

Ambrose. *On the Christian Faith*. In *Nicene and Post-Nicene Fathers*, edited by Philip Schaff and Henry Wace, 2nd ser., 10:199–314. Reprint, Grand Rapids: Eerdmans, 1983.

Aquinas, Thomas. *Summa Theologica*. Translated by Fathers of the English Dominican Province. New York: Benziger Brothers, 1911–25.

Athanasius. *On the Incarnation*. Translated by John Behr. Crestwood, NY: St. Vladimir's Seminary Press, 2012.

Auden, W. H. "As I Walked Out One Evening." In *W. H. Auden: Collected Poems*, edited by Edward Mendelson, 135. New York: Random House, 1991.

Augustine. *Confessions*. Translated by Henry Chadwick. New York: Oxford University Press, 2008.

———. *On Christian Belief*. Translated by Edmund Hill et al. The Works of Saint Augustine I/8. Hyde Park, NY: New City, 2005.

———. *On Christian Teaching*. Translated by R. P. H. Green. New York: Oxford University Press, 2008.

———. *Soliloquies: Augustine's Inner Dialogue*. Translated by Kim Paffenroth. Hyde Park, NY: New City, 2000.

Bahnson, Fred. "Guardians of Memory." *Harper's Magazine*, August 2022. https://harpers.org/archive/2022/08/the-quest-to-save-ancient-manuscripts-gao-mali/.

———. *Soil and Sacrament*. New York: Simon & Schuster, 2013.

———. "Unbroken Grace." *Emergence Magazine*, December 21, 2021. https://emergencemagazine.org/essay/an-unbroken-grace/.

Baldwin, James. "*The Black Scholar* Interviews James Baldwin." In *Conversations with James Baldwin*, edited by Fred L. Standley and Louis H. Pratt, 142–58. Jackson: University Press of Mississippi, 1989.

Barron, Robert. *The Strangest Way: Walking the Christian Path*. New York: Orbis, 2003.

Basil the Great. *On Social Justice*. Translated by C. Paul Schroeder. Crestwood, NY: St. Vladimir's Seminary Press, 2009.

———. *The Rule of St. Basil in Latin and English: A Revised Critical Edition*. Translated by Anna M. Silvas. Collegeville, MN: Liturgical Press, 2013.

———. *Saint Basil: Ascetical Works*. Translated by M. Monica Wagner. Fathers of the Church. Washington, DC: Catholic University of America Press, 1950.

Bell, Luke. *The Meaning of Blue: Recovering a Contemplative Spirit*. Kettering, OH: Second Spring, 2014.

Bellah, Robert N., Richard Madsen, William Sullivan, Ann Swidler, and Steven Tipton. *Habits of the Heart: Individualism and Commitment in American Life*. Berkeley: University of California Press, 1985.

Bennett, Kyle. *Practices of Love: Spiritual Disciplines for the Life of the World*. Grand Rapids: Brazos, 2017.

Berry, Wendell. *Jayber Crow*. Berkeley: Counterpoint, 2000.

———. *Life Is a Miracle: An Essay on Modern Superstition*. Berkeley: Counterpoint, 2001.

———. "The Native Grasses and What They Mean." *New Farm*, 1980, 50–57.

———. *The Unsettling of America: Culture and Agriculture*. New York: Avon, 1978.

Blamires, Harry. *The Christian Mind: How Should a Christian Think?* Ann Arbor, MI: Servant, 1963.

Boersma, Hans. "A Sacramental Journey to the Beatific Vision: The Intellectualism of Pierre Rousselot." *Heythrop Journal* 49 (2008): 1015–34.

———. *Seeing God: The Beatific Vision in the Christian Tradition.* Grand Rapids: Eerdmans, 2018.

Bonhoeffer, Dietrich. *Berlin: 1932–1933.* Edited by Larry Rasmussen. Translated by Isabel Best, David Higgins, and Douglas Stott. Dietrich Bonhoeffer Works 12. Minneapolis: Fortress, 2009.

———. *Christ the Center.* Translated by Edwin H. Robertson. New York: Harper & Row, 1960.

———. "The Church and the Jewish Question." In *No Rusty Swords: Letters, Lectures and Notes, 1928–1936,* 224–26. Translated by Edwin H. Robertson and John Bowden. New York: Harper & Row, 1965.

———. *Discipleship.* Edited by Geffrey B. Kelly and John D. Godsey. Translated by Barbara Green and Reinhard Krauss. Dietrich Bonhoeffer Works 4. Minneapolis: Fortress, 2001.

———. *Letters and Papers from Prison.* Edited by Eberhard Bethge. Translated by Reginald Fuller. New York: Macmillan, 1967.

———. *Life Together.* Translated by John W. Doberstein. New York: Harper & Row, 1954.

———. *Prayerbook of the Bible.* In *Life Together, Prayerbook of the Bible,* edited by Geffrey B. Kelly and translated by Daniel W. Bloesch and James H. Burtness, 141–77. Dietrich Bonhoeffer Works 5. Minneapolis: Fortress, 2005.

———. *Sanctorum Communio: A Theological Study of the Sociology of the Church.* Edited by Clifford J. Green. Translated by Reinhard Krauss and Nancy Lukens. Dietrich Bonhoeffer Works 1. Minneapolis: Fortress, 1998.

———. *A Testament to Freedom.* Edited by Jeffrey Kellyard and R. Burton Nelson. San Francisco: Harper & Row, 1990.

Bosanquet, Mary. *The Life and Death of Dietrich Bonhoeffer.* New York: Harper & Row, 1968.

Brooks, David. *The Road to Character.* New York: Random House, 2016.

———. "The Ultimate Spoiler Alert." Commencement address at Dartmouth University, Hanover, New Hampshire, June 14, 2015. https://news.dartmouth.edu/news/2015/06/david-brooks-commencement-address.

Brown, Peter. *Augustine of Hippo: A Biography.* Berkeley: University of California Press, 1967.

Buechner, Frederick. *Wishful Thinking: A Seeker's ABC.* New York: Harper & Row, 1973.

Calvin, John. *Institutes of the Christian Religion.* Translated by Henry Beveridge. Peabody, MA: Hendrickson, 2008.

Capon, Robert Farrar. *Between Noon and Three: Romance, Law, and the Outrage of Grace.* Grand Rapids: Eerdmans, 1997.

Cassian, John. *The Conferences.* Translated by Colm Luibheid. New York: Paulist Press, 1985.

Charry, Ellen. *By the Renewing of Your Minds: The Pastoral Function of Christian Doctrine.* New York: Oxford University Press, 1997.

Chesterton, G. K. *Orthodoxy.* New York: Image, 1908.

The Cloud of Unknowing. Translated by A. C. Spearing. Harmondsworth, UK: Penguin, 2001.

Craft, Jennifer Allen. *Placemaking and the Arts: Cultivating the Christian Life.* Downers Grove, IL: IVP Academic, 2018.

Dailey, Hannah. "Taylor Swift's NYU Commencement Speech: Read the Full Transcript." *Billboard,* May 15, 2022. https://www.billboard.com/music/music-news/taylor-swift-nyu-commencement-speech-full-transcript-1235072824/.

Day, Dorothy. *The Duty of Delight: The Diaries of Dorothy Day.* Edited by Robert Ellsberg. New York: Image, 2011.

———. *The Long Loneliness: The Autobiography of the Legendary Catholic Social Activist.* New York: Harper & Brothers, 1952.

de Gruchy, John W. *Christianity, Art and Transformation: Theological Aesthetics in the Struggle for Justice.* Cambridge: Cambridge University Press, 2011.

Dodson, Jonathan. *Gospel-Centered Discipleship.* Wheaton: Crossway, 2022.

Eisenhower, Dwight D. *At Ease: Stories I Tell to Friends.* New York: Doubleday, 1967.

Eliot, T. S. *Four Quartets.* New York: Harcourt, Brace, 1943.

Espín, Orlando O., and James B. Nickoloff. *An Introductory Dictionary of Theology and Religious Studies.* Collegeville, MN: Liturgical Press, 2007.

Evagrius of Pontus. *The Praktikos and Chapters on Prayer.* Translated by John Eudes Bamberger. Collegeville, MN: Cistercian Publications, 1972.

Fabrycky, Laura M. *Keys to Bonhoeffer's Haus: Exploring the World and Wisdom of Dietrich Bonhoeffer.* Minneapolis: Fortress, 2020.

Fujimura, Makoto. *Art and Faith: A Theology of Making.* New Haven: Yale University Press, 2020.

Garrigou-Lagrange, Réginald. *The Three Ages of the Interior Life*, vol. 1. Translated by M. Timothea Doyle. St. Louis: B. Herder, 1960.

Gilson, Étienne. *The Christian Philosophy of Saint Augustine*. London: Victor Gollancz, 1961.

Gioia, Dana. "Christianity and Poetry." *First Things*, August 2022. https://www.firstthings.com/article/2022/08/christianity-and-poetry.

Godspeed: The Pace of Being Known. Directed by Danny Lund. Ranch Studios. 2017. 36:53. https://www.livegodspeed.org/watchgodspeed.

González, Justo. *The Mestizo Augustine: A Theologian between Two Cultures*. Downers Grove, IL: IVP Academic, 2016.

Gregory of Nyssa. *The Life of Moses*. Translated by Abraham J. Malherbe and Everett Ferguson. Mahwah, NJ: Paulist Press, 1978.

———. *On Perfection*. In *St. Gregory of Nyssa: Ascetical Works*, translated by Virginia Callahan, 121–22. Fathers of the Church. Washington, DC: Catholic University of America Press, 1967.

Guinness, Os. *Fit Bodies, Fat Minds: Why Evangelicals Don't Think and What to Do about It*. Grand Rapids: Hourglass, 1994.

Hart, David Bentley. "The Offering of Names: Metaphysics, Nihilism, and Analogy." In *The Hidden and the Manifest: Essays in Theology and Metaphysics*, 1–44. Grand Rapids: Eerdmans, 2017.

Hauerwas, Stanley. "Christian Practice and the Practice of Law in a World without Foundations." *Mercer Law Review* 44, no. 3 (1993): 748–60.

———. *A Community of Character: Toward a Constructive Christian Social Ethic*. Notre Dame, IN: University of Notre Dame Press, 1991.

———. "The End of American Protestantism." Religion and Ethics. ABC (website). July 2, 2013. https://www.abc.net.au/religion/the-end-of-american-protestantism/10099770.

———. *In Good Company: The Church as Polis*. Notre Dame, IN: University of Notre Dame Press, 1995.

———. *Working with Words: On Learning to Speak Christian*. Eugene, OR: Cascade Books, 2011.

Hauerwas, Stanley, and William Willimon. "The Dangers of Providing Pastoral Care." *Christian Century*, July 27, 2021. https://www.christiancentury.org/article/interview/dangers-providing-pastoral-care.

Haynes, Stephen R. *The Bonhoeffer Phenomenon: Portraits of a Protestant Saint*. Minneapolis: Fortress, 2004.

Herdt, Jennifer. *Putting on Virtue: The Legacy of the Splendid Vices.* Chicago: University of Chicago Press, 2008.

Heschel, Abraham. *Between God and Man: An Interpretation of Judaism.* New York: Free Press, 1997.

———. *The Sabbath.* New York: Farrar, Straus & Giroux, 2005.

Horton, Michael. *The Christian Faith: A Systematic Theology for Pilgrims on the Way.* Grand Rapids: Zondervan Academic, 2011.

Hunter, George, III. *The Celtic Way of Evangelism: How Christianity Can Reach the West . . . Again.* Nashville: Abingdon, 2000.

Irenaeus. *Against Heresies.* Translated by John Keble. Delafield, WI: Nashotah House Press, 2012.

Isaac the Syrian. *Mystic Treatises of Isaac of Nineveh.* Translated by A. J. Wensinck. Amsterdam: Uitgave der Koninklijke Akademie van Wetenschappen, 1923.

Jacobs, Alan. *Breaking Bread with the Dead: A Reader's Guide to a More Tranquil Mind.* New York: Penguin, 2020.

Jensen, Robin M. *The Substance of Things Seen: Art, Faith, and the Christian Community.* Grand Rapids: Eerdmans, 2004.

John of the Cross. *Dark Night of the Soul.* Translated by David Lewis. Charlotte: Tan Books, 2010.

———. "Maxim on Love, 88." In *The Collected Works of St. John of the Cross,* translated by K. Kavanaugh and O. Rodriguez, 92. Washington, DC: Institute of Carmelite Studies, 1979.

Johnson, Dru. *Scripture's Knowing: A Companion to Biblical Epistemology.* Eugene, OR: Cascade Books, 2015.

Keating, Thomas. *Intimacy with God: An Introduction to Centering Prayer.* New York: Crossroad, 2009.

King, Martin Luther, Jr. "Three Dimensions of a Complete Life." Sermon at the Unitarian Church of Germantown, Pennsylvania, December 11, 1960. Available at the Martin Luther King, Jr. Research and Education Institute. Stanford University (website). https://kinginstitute.stanford.edu/king-papers/documents/three-dimensions-complete-life-sermon-delivered-unitarian-church-germantown.

Kreeft, Peter. "Beauty Is the First Thing We Notice and Love." Interview by Paul Senz. *Catholic World Report,* May 1, 2020. https://www.catholicworldreport.com/2020/05/01/dr-peter-kreeft-beauty-is-the-first-thing-we-notice-and-love/.

Laird, Martin. *Into the Silent Land: A Guide to the Christian Practice of Contemplation*. New York: Oxford University Press, 2006.

Lancashire, Ian, ed. "A Fruitful Exhortation to the Reading of Holy Scripture." Anglican Library (website). 1994. http://www.anglicanlibrary.org/homilies/bk1hom01.htm.

Lewis, C. S. *The Collected Letters of C. S. Lewis*, vol. 1. Edited by Walter Hooper. San Francisco: HarperOne, 2004.

———. *The Great Divorce*. In *The Complete C. S. Lewis Signature Classics*, 311–64. New York: HarperCollins, 2002.

———. *Made for Heaven*. New York: HarperCollins, 2005.

———. *Mere Christianity*. San Francisco: HarperOne, 2001.

Lossky, Vladimir. *The Mystical Theology of the Eastern Church*. Crestwood, NY: St. Vladimir's Seminary Press, 1957.

Lovelace, Richard. *Renewal as a Way of Life: A Guidebook for Spiritual Growth*. Eugene, OR: Wipf & Stock, 2002.

Luther, Martin. *A Commentary on St. Paul's Epistle to the Galatians*. Philadelphia: Smith, English & Co., 1860.

MacIntyre, Alasdair. *After Virtue: A Study in Moral Theory*. Notre Dame, IN: Notre Dame University Press, 1984.

Mawson, Michael. *Christ Existing as Community: Bonhoeffer's Ecclesiology*. New York: Oxford University Press, 2018.

Mayfield, D. L. *The Unruly Saint: Dorothy Day's Radical Vision and Its Challenge for Our Times*. Minneapolis: Broadleaf, 2022.

McDermott, John. *Love and Understanding: The Relation of Will and Intellect in Pierre Rousselot's Christological Vision*. Analecta Gregoriana 229. Rome: Università Gregoriana Editrice, 1983.

Merton, Thomas. *A Course in Christian Mysticism*. Edited by Jon M. Sweeney. Collegeville, MN: Liturgical Press, 2017.

———. *New Seeds of Contemplation*. New York: New Directions, 1961.

———. *No Man Is an Island*. New York: HarperOne, 2002.

———. *The Seven Storey Mountain: An Autobiography of Faith*. New York: Harcourt, 1948.

Milliner, Matthew. "Becoming Bourbon." *Image Journal* 101 (Winter 2021). https://imagejournal.org/article/becoming-bourbon/.

Mohler, Albert. "Nearing the End—a Conversation with Theologian Stanley Hauerwas." *Thinking in Public* (podcast), April 28, 2014. Recording and transcript at https://albertmohler.com/2014/04/28/nearing-the-end-a-con versation-with-theologian-stanley-hauerwas.

———. "The Scandal of Biblical Illiteracy: It's Our Problem." AlbertMohler .com, January 20, 2016. https://albertmohler.com/2016/01/20/the-scandal -of-biblical-illiteracy-its-our-problem-4/.

Moreland, J. P. *Love Your God with All Your Mind: The Role of Reason in the Life of the Soul.* Colorado Springs: NavPress, 1997.

Nicholas of Cusa. *On the Vision of God.* Translated by Emma Gurney Salter. New York: Cosimo Classics, 2007.

Niebuhr, Richard. *The Kingdom of God in America.* Middletown, CT: Wesleyan University Press, 1988.

Noll, Mark. *The Scandal of the Evangelical Mind.* Grand Rapids: Eerdmans, 2022.

Nouwen, Henri. *Life of the Beloved.* New York: Crossroad, 1992.

Nwigwe, Tobe. "I CHOOSE YOU." Track 7 on *THE ORIGINALS.* No label, 2018.

Oberman, Heiko A. *Luther: Man between God and the Devil.* New Haven: Yale University Press, 2006.

Oden, Thomas C., and Christopher A. Hall, eds. *Mark.* Ancient Christian Commentary on Scripture. Downers Grove, IL: InterVarsity, 1998.

O'Malley, Timothy. "Why Americans Struggle to Understand Catholicism." Church Life Journal, January 24, 2022. https://churchlifejournal.nd.edu /articles/why-americans-struggle-to-understand-catholicism/.

Otto, Rudolf. *The Idea of the Holy.* Translated by John W. Harvey. Oxford: Oxford University Press, 1928.

Palmer, Parker. *To Know as We Are Known: Education as a Spiritual Journey.* San Francisco: HarperSanFrancisco, 1983.

Pascal, Blaise. *Pensées.* Translated by A. J. Krailsheimer. New York: Penguin Classics, 1995.

Pink, A. W. *Profiting from the Word of God.* London: Banner of Truth, 1981.

———. *Spiritual Growth.* Grand Rapids: Baker Books, 1971.

Pohl, Christine D. *Living into Community: Cultivating Practices That Sustain Us.* Grand Rapids: Eerdmans, 2012.

Putnam, Robert D. *Bowling Alone: The Collapse and Revival of American Community.* New York: Simon & Schuster, 2000.

Roberts, Nancy. *Dorothy Day and the* Catholic Worker. New York: Orbis Books, 2011.

Robinson, Marilynne. *The Death of Adam: Essays on Modern Thought*. New York: Picador, 2005.

Rohr, Richard. *Falling Upward: A Spirituality for the Two Halves of Life*. San Francisco: Jossey-Bass, 2011.

Rolheiser, Ronald. *Domestic Monastery: Creating a Spiritual Life at Home*. Brewster, MA: Paraclete, 2019.

————. *The Holy Longing: The Search for a Christian Spirituality*. New York: Doubleday, 1999.

Saward, John. *Perfect Fools: Folly for Christ's Sake in Catholic and Orthodox Spirituality*. Oxford: Oxford University Press, 2000.

Sayers, Dorothy. *Letters to a Diminished Church: Passionate Arguments for the Relevance of Christian Doctrine*. Nashville: Nelson, 2004.

The Sayings of the Desert Fathers. Translated by Benedicta Ward. Kalamazoo, MI: Cistercian Publications, 1975.

Schmemann, Alexander. *For the Life of the World*. Yonkers, NY: St. Vladimir's Seminary Press, 2018.

Smith, Christian, with Melinda Lundquist Denton. *Soul Searching: The Religious and Spiritual Lives of American Teenagers*. Oxford: Oxford University Press, 2005.

Smith, James K. A. *On the Road with St. Augustine: A Real-World Spirituality for Restless Hearts*. Grand Rapids: Brazos, 2019.

Smither, Edward L. *Mission in the Early Church: Themes and Reflections*. Eugene, OR: Cascade Books, 2014.

Sosler, Alex. "Attentional Arts and Beholding Beauty." Front Porch Republic, March 9, 2022. https://www.frontporchrepublic.com/2022/03/attentional-arts-and-beholding-beauty/.

Sullivan, Shirley Darcus. *Transformed by Love: The Soul's Journey to God*. Hyde Park, NY: New City, 2022.

Taylor, Charles. *The Ethics of Authenticity*. Cambridge, MA: Harvard University Press, 2018.

————. *Sources of the Self*. Cambridge: Cambridge University Press, 1992.

Teresa of Ávila. *Book of the Foundations*. Translated by John Dalton. London: Paternoster, 1853.

————. *The Interior Castle*. Translated by Kieran Kavanaugh and Otilio Rodriguez. Mahwah, NJ: Paulist Press, 1979.

————. *The Life of Saint Teresa of Avila*. Translated by J. M. Cohen. New York: Penguin, 1957.

Thérèse of Lisieux. *Letters of St. Therese of Lisieux*. Translated by John Clarke. Washington, DC: ICS Publications, 1982.

Thompson, Gregory. "To Inhabit the Earth." *Comment Magazine*, October 1, 2022. https://comment.org/to-inhabit-the-earth/.

von Balthasar, Hans Urs. *Explorations in Theology*. Vol. 1, *The Word Made Flesh*. San Francisco: Ignatius, 2011.

Warren, Tish Harrison. *Liturgy of the Ordinary: Sacred Practices in Everyday Life*. Downers Grove, IL: InterVarsity, 2016.

———. *Prayer in the Night: For Those Who Work or Watch or Weep*. Downers Grove, IL: InterVarsity, 2021.

Werntz, Myles. *From Isolation to Community: A Renewed Vision for Christian Life Together*. Grand Rapids: Baker Academic, 2022.

———. "Making Little of the Law and Everything of Love." *Comment Magazine*, March 17, 2022. https://comment.org/making-little-of-the-law-and-everything-of-love/.

Wickenden, Dorothy. "Wendell Berry's Advice for a Cataclysmic Age." *New Yorker*, February 21, 2022. https://www.newyorker.com/magazine/2022/02/28/wendell-berrys-advice-for-a-cataclysmic-age.

Williams, Rowan. *Holy Living: The Christian Tradition for Today*. New York: Bloomsbury Continuum, 2017.

———. *Looking East in Winter: Contemporary Thought and the Eastern Christian Tradition*. London: Bloomsbury, 2021.

———. *Teresa of Avila*. New York: Continuum, 1991.

———. *Wrestling with Angels: Conversations in Modern Theology*. Grand Rapids: Eerdmans, 2007.

Wirzba, Norman. *Agrarian Spirit: Cultivating Faith, Community, and the Land*. Notre Dame, IN: University of Notre Dame Press, 2022.

Wright, N. T. *After You Believe: Why Christian Character Matters*. San Francisco: HarperOne, 2012.

Index